TEXTILES ● U. K.‑IRELAND

English embroidery of the 16–17th Century. Silk on velvet, for a bed hanging. *Victoria & Albert (V & A)* — GX 3174 *(no acc. number).*

Woven in silk at Coventry, 1863–4, to commemorate the marriage of the Prince of Wales to a Danish princess. Coventry was famous during the 19th Century for its woven silk ribbons and pictures. This tour de force shows why. *V & A — FG 1685 (373-1864).*

TEXTILE COLLECTIONS OF THE WORLD

●

VOL. 2

UNITED KINGDOM-IRELAND

EDITOR : CECIL LUBELL

AN ILLUSTRATED GUIDE TO TEXTILE COLLECTIONS
IN THE UNITED KINGDOM AND IRELAND

Studio Vista
London

A Studio Vista book published by
Cassell & Collier Macmillan Publishers Ltd,
35 Red Lion Square, London WC1R 4SG
and at Sydney, Auckland, Toronto, Johannesburg
and affiliate of
Macmillan Publishing Co. Inc.,
New York.

Printed in the United States

English embroidered panel of the mid-17th Century. Silk petit point on linen. *Whitworth — W. 385 (8828). Cox Bequest, 1910.*

Scottish woven wool shawl, about 1860. Possibly from Paisley. 11½ x 5½ feet. *Royal Scottish — 1922.559. MacFarlane Gift.*

Plan and Purpose

The *Textile Collections of the World* series combines resource information with design ideas.

As such, they are chiefly directed to professional textile designers, to producers of textiles, to craft workers in thread, and to students of textile design.

Resource information is given in reviews of the textile collections.

Textile-design ideas are shown in color and B/W photos of pieces in the collections reviewed.

Photos are arranged in historical sequence. But the intent was not to present a picture history of textile design, with all stages represented. That would have meant showing many designs for their historical import rather than for their visual impact on contemporary designers. It would also have involved the repetition of basic design themes, which surface at different times in many places.

This I have sought to avoid. My aim has been to select pictures which show graphic ideas that I consider adaptable to today's textiles. The photos thus reflect a personal view of the collections.

My hope is that these reviews and this photographic sampling will prod designers into visiting the museums and exploring the source material for themselves. — C.L.

Contents • Vol. 2 • U. K.-Ireland

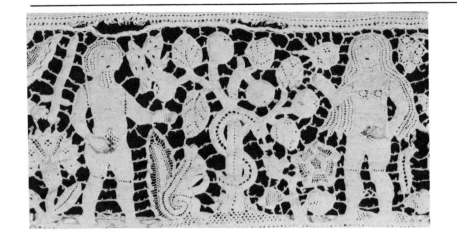

English sampler of the 17th Century.
The Adam & Eve story in needlepoint lace,
done with childlike directness.
Fitzwilliam — 3678 (T3-1938). Longman Bequest.

INTRODUCTION

Look at a map of the world.

The United Kingdom and Ireland lie off the Northwest corner of Europe — two small islands almost lost on the vast surface of the globe. They cover an area of 121,000 square miles and are home to 59 million people — minor fragments of the world's 52 million square miles and 3.7 billion inhabitants but a major factor in the history of world textiles.

Think of the fabrics we wear today or those we use to furnish our homes. A disproportionate number originated in these small, textile-intensive islands.

Clan Tartans and District Checks . . . Harris, Shetland, and Donegal tweeds . . . worsted suitings from Yorkshire . . . patterned shirtings from Lancashire . . . Foulard-tie prints and Liberty silks . . . Paisley and Norwich shawls . . . weaving from Spitalfields and Macclesfield . . . Elizabethan embroidery . . . Irish linen and lace . . . Nottingham machine lace . . . crewelwork . . . Axminster and Wilton carpets . . . English flannel . . . Jersey . . . Oxford cloth . . . Tattersall checks . . . Poplin . . . sheep breeds whose names are largely English . . . textile machinery whose basic inventions were made by Englishmen — Kay, Wyatt, Paul, Lee, Strutt, Hargreaves, Arkwright, and Compton.

These terms and these names made textile history. They represented a major factor in the industrial growth of these islands, and they fostered an interest in fabric which is reflected today in many museum collections scattered throughout the region.

More than forty such collections of textiles are reviewed in this volume. Many of them are not large, but all hold interest for designers and students. Each offers the visitor some area of specialization or some ambience which makes it different from other collections.

One is very large and dominant on the scene. The Department of Textiles at the Victoria & Albert Museum in London is one of the largest and most influential facility of this kind in the world.

I have a recurring image about the V & A. It seems to sit like a brood hen over the decorative-arts departments of almost all museums in the U. K. This is not meant invidiously but in admiration for the competence, the authority, and the resources of the V & A as a na-

Scottish sampler dated 1822. Linen embroidered with silk threads, mostly cross-stitch. *Royal Scottish — 1923.565.*

English embroidered picture from the first half of the 18th Century. Yarns are wool and silk on linen ground. *Royal Scottish — 1945.4547.*

English embroidered panel of the late 16th Century. It is worked in silks and gold/silver yarns in a repeat pattern. The vineline structure is typical of Elizabethan embroidery work. *Burrell Collection — 29/16.*

English, late 17th Century. An embroidered man's cap with the vinelike structure noted in the earlier piece, above. Silk and metal yarns are used in many different stitches on the linen ground cloth. *Fitzwilliam — 267 (T9-1947). Clarke Bequest.*

English crewelwork curtain, dated 1696. The embroidery is worked with worsted yarns on a cotton/linen twill-weave cloth. Some twelve different stitches are used. *V & A — Y499 (T166-1961).*

INTRODUCTION Con't

tional institution. At almost every museum you visit in the British Isles, you meet "graduates" of the V & A. It has served as the incubator, the training ground for staff members in museums throughout the country. Its own keepers (curators) are looked up to as authorities in their specialized fields and their expertise is constantly reinforced through travel, study, and contact with other museums around the world.

Because the V & A occupies so dominant a position, other textile collections in the U. K. and Ireland are inevitably overshadowed. But this does not mean that they lack interest for designers and students of textile design.

In London itself the British Museum's Ethnology Department (Museum of Mankind) and the Horniman Museum both hold "primitive" textiles not represented in the V & A collection. The Bethnal Green Museum, the Museum of London, the Gunnersbury Park Museum, and the William Morris Gallery are four other museums in London which hold small textile collections and which should interest designers because of the special areas on which they focus attention. And there is a small but very rewarding research collection of sample books at London's Royal College of Art.

Beyond London there are some thirty textile collections easily reached by train in this region of short distances. (For foreign visitors the Britrail Pass is an open sesame.)

The museums at Bath, Bedford, Norwich, and Reading can each be examined in a day's journey-and-return from London. The emphasis in these museums is on costume, but each owns related flat fabrics, and designers will find the collections rewarding. Close to Bath is the Welsh Folk Museum near Cardiff, with its 18th-Century woolen mill. Cambridge and Oxford are each about an hour's train ride from London, and each contains small but important collections of textiles, particularly in the ethnological area.

Somewhat farther North — but still within two to three hours by train from London — are the collections at Nottingham, Liverpool, and Manchester. Nottingham specializes in lace. Liverpool holds the girdle of Ramses III (12th Century B.C.), which should be seen by all textile designers and craft weavers if only for the humility it will inspire. Manchester has the Whitworth Gallery — the second most

English woven cloth, dated 1765–8.
Detail of a brocaded-silk dress fabric
with a three-dimensional effect achieved
through the background striping.
V & A — GA 304 (T44-1912).

important textile collection in the U. K. — as well as the Gallery of English Costume. It is a must on any designer's itinerary.

In close and logical proximity to this center of the Lancashire textile industry are the museums at Bolton, Blackburn, and Halifax — each an interesting attempt to show the effects of the industrial revolution on textiles. Halifax, particularly, has a unique resource for hand-weavers in its Bankfield Museum.

Continuing north, there is a small but choice collection of Far Eastern fabrics at the Gulbenkian Museum in Durham and an equally choice group of Mediterranean embroideries at the Laing Art Gallery in Newcastle-Upon-Tyne.

Scotland has notable collections in both Glasgow and Edinburgh. In Glasgow there is the Burrell Collection, famous for its tapestries and carpets, and the Art Gallery & Museum at Kelvingrove, which has a substantial costume collection and plans to expand into contemporary textiles. Nearby, there is a fine exhibit of shawls at Paisley and the historically interesting Weaver's Cottage at Kilbarchan.

In Edinburgh, the Royal Scottish Museum holds one of the major textile collections in the U. K. — much of it on display in the handsome, skylit, Crystal Palace interior hall. Edinburgh also has the National Museum of Antiquities, with an important collection of early printwork sample books and Scottish tartans. For tartan researchers the world's largest and most authoritative collection of Clan tartans is also in Scotland, at Broughty Castle in Dundee.

In Northern Ireland the Ulster Museum in Belfast and the Ulster Folk Museum in nearby Holywood both hold important and diversified collections of textiles and costume.

In the Republic of Ireland the National Museum in Dublin has an excellent study collection of textiles from many cultures and periods as well as a fine collection of Irish and European lace. Seventy miles south of Dublin is the Kilkenny Design Workshop. Though it is not a museum, it represents an important source of textile design in Ireland and is therefore worthy of mention in this review.

At most of these institutions I have been impressed with the degree of attention given to textiles by the authorities in charge. Perhaps I am reading too much into this, but I see in it a reflection of the important role textiles have played in the culture of these islands — not only the textiles produced here but also the vastly different and more exotic fabrics of far distant lands, which have been absorbed into the cultural patterns of these island people.

Detail from a fragment of brocaded silk,
woven about 1730, probably in the
Spitalfields district of London.
V & A — R 251 (T75-1936).

Design for a printed shawl, probably made in Paisley, Scotland between 1840–55. This is pattern #5091 from a book of print proofs owned by the National Museum of Antiquities of Scotland.

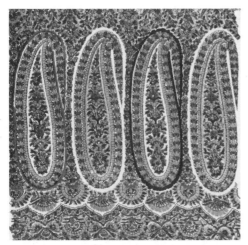

Pattern #4078 from the same book of proofs noted above. This is a border print and the pine-cone ("paisley") motif is a little over six inches in height.

A woven Paisley shawl of cream-colored wool, made in Scotland between 1860–70 when the Paisley industry dominated the field. This one is about 5½ feet square. *Royal Scottish — 1947.135. McBain Bequest.*

INTRODUCTION Con't

Every exploration has a human dimension. The individuals you meet, the way you interact with them, the warmth of their reception, their interest in your work — these subtle nuances can lift an experience from routine into pleasure. In this I was fortunate. The pleasurable meetings were more numerous than the routine ones, and I would like here to express my gratitude to the museum people who made them so.

To Donald King, Natalie Rothstein, and Andrew Dempsey of the V & A, for their interest in my work and their indispensable assistance in exploring the vast resources of their museum; to Robin Crighton and Jane Palmer of the Fitzwilliam Museum, for friendliness far beyond the call of duty; to Revel Oddy of the Royal Scottish Museum, for making my visit to Edinburgh so rewarding; to William Wells and Brian Blench, for making me feel at home in Glasgow; to Margaret Warhurst, for sharing her Liverpool treasures with me; to my friend Roger Nicholson, for uncovering design resources at the Royal College of Art; to Kay Staniland of the London Museum, for a friendly morning; to Joan Allgrove of the Whitworth Gallery, for the warmth of her welcome and her unstinting cooperation; to Oliver Snoddy of the National Museum in Dublin, for an interesting morning and a new insight into James Joyce; to Mortimer O'Shea of the Kilkenny Design Workshops, for encouragement and intelligent suggestions; to versatile Myra Mines at the Bath Museum of Costume, for the pleasure of meeting her again; to Winnie Grygierczyk, photo printer at the V & A, whose fine craftsmanship and hard work made it possible for me to leave London with the pictures I wanted; and, not least, to my transplanted son Stephen Lubell, for his assistance in assembling materials for this book.

I wish also to thank the many museum staff members not mentioned here by name, whose interest and knowledge made this work possible and rewarding.

Finally, I would like to record my special debt of gratitude to Natalie Rothstein for her fine and scholarly essay on the History of British Textile Design — an invaluable contribution to this volume.

Cecil Lubell
Croton-on-Hudson, N.Y.
December, 1975

U.K.–IRELAND

GUIDE TO THE COLLECTIONS

SEQUENCE IS ARRANGED IN ALPHABETICAL ORDER BY CITY.

BATH — The American Museum in Britain

BATH — The Museum of Costume

BEDFORD — The Cecil Higgins Art Gallery

BELFAST — Richard Atkinson & Co.

BELFAST — Ulster Museum

BLACKBURN — Lewis Textile Museum

BOLTON — Museum & Art Gallery

CAMBRIDGE — Fitzwilliam Museum

CAMBRIDGE — University Museum

CARDIFF — Welsh Folk Museum

DUBLIN — National Museum of Ireland

DUNDEE — The Scottish Tartans Society

DURHAM — Gulbenkian Museum of Oriental Art

EDINBURGH — "Our Scottish District Checks"

EDINBURGH — National Museum of Antiquities

EDINBURGH — Royal Scottish Museum

GLASGOW — Art Gallery & Museum

GLASGOW — The Burrell Collection

GLASGOW — The Hunterian Museum

HALIFAX — Bankfield Museum

HOLYWOOD — Ulster Folk Museum

KILBARCHAN — The Weaver's Cottage

KILKENNY — Kilkenny Design Workshops

LIVERPOOL — Merseyside County Museums

LONDON — Bethnal Green Museum

LONDON — The British Museum

LONDON — Gunnersbury Park Museum

LONDON — Horniman Museum & Library

LONDON — The Museum of London

LONDON — William Morris Gallery

LONDON — Museum of Mankind

LONDON — Royal College of Art

LONDON — Victoria & Albert Museum

MANCHESTER — The Gallery of English Costume

MANCHESTER — The Whitworth Gallery

NEWCASTLE UPON TYNE — Laing Art Gallery

NORWICH — Strangers' Hall Museum

NOTTINGHAM — Castle Museum & Art Gallery

OXFORD — The Ashmolean Museum

OXFORD — Pitt Rivers Museum

PAISLEY — Museum & Art Galleries

READING — Museum of English Rural Life

LEFT. The Assembly Rooms, Bath, in which the Museum of Costume is housed. The interior shows part of the draper's shop display (Scene 6) with its silk-ribbon sample book, c. 1862.

BELOW. Closeup of a page from the 1862 ribbon sample book. *Museum of Costume.*

BATH

The American Museum in Britain
Claverton Manor   BA2 7BD
TEL: Bath 60503

Shiela Betterton, Textile Advisor

The American Museum in Britain is housed in a handsome manor house set in lovely gardens on a hill with a sweeping view of rolling countryside and the city of Bath. It is easily reached on Bus 217 from a stop near the Bath Abbey.

The museum shows some aspects of American life styles from the 17th to the 19th Century. The furnished rooms will seem quite familiar to Americans but not to Europeans. It also displays artifacts of the American Indians, the Shakers, the Pennsylvania Dutch, and the Spanish colonists in New Mexico.

But for textile designers and students the main attraction is an impressive collection of American quilts and coverlets. The museum owns over 100 pieces, and most are conveniently displayed on large, hinged panels — the way rugs are often arranged in a department store.

The collection includes patchwork, appliqué, quilting, candlewick and embroidered spreads, as well as stuffed work, or "trapunto." Woven coverlets range from simple twill-weave blankets to more sophisticated jacquards. There are also a number of hooked rugs and a rare needlework bed rug dated 1833. Some crewelwork is shown in 18th-Century bed hangings and curtains.

Publication. "American Textiles and Needlework" by Shiela Betterton (40 pages). An excellent booklet on early home crafts in America. It discusses coverlets, rugs, crewelwork, and Indian crafts in terms of their history and design development. The techniques used are clearly described.

BATH

The Museum of Costume
Assembly Rooms, Alfred St.
TEL: Bath 28411, Ext. 298

Myra E. Mines, Chief Costume Asst.

The city of Bath has no textile collection as such, but it does have a notable museum of costume which shows some flat textiles in its permanent displays and holds a fair-sized group in reserve storage. Bath is also one of the most pleasant cities in England to visit.

The Museum is housed in the imposing Assembly Rooms and deserves more space and attention that the city fathers see fit to assign it. Even so, it is considered to be the largest permanent display of costume in the world. It exhibits some 200 clothes manikins, many in room settings of specific periods, and it has detailed displays of such garments as underwear and children's clothes. It covers a time span from 1580 to the present and holds annual exhibits of contemporary "Clothes of the Year."

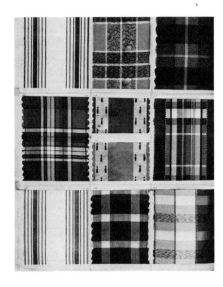

For textile designers it has one exceptional treasure. This is a large sample book of woven silk ribbons assembled about 1862 and exhibited at the Crystal Palace International Exhibition of that year in London. The book contains at least 1,500 samples, including a large group of tartans in silk taffeta. It is full of rich design material for both woven and printed textiles.

The ribbon sample book can be examined on request. It is interestingly displayed behind glass in the setting of a draper's shop where such ribbons were sold in the mid-19th Century (Scene 6).

The museum also holds in reserve a large and varied collection of shawls, chiefly 19th Century, many from the looms of Paisley and Norwich. Its collection of embroidered men's waistcoats is also exceptional.

The museum was founded by Doris Langley Moore, whose private collection was its core. It has now been greatly expanded through new bequests and is ably administered by Myra E. Mines, who began her career as a costume restorer and knows her collection from the inside out.

Research Center. As of June, 1974, The Museum of Costume opened a new "Costume & Fashion Research Centre" in one of the elegant 18th-Century town houses on The Circus — a few minutes' walk from the museum. The five floors of the house have been handsomely converted into library, study room, lecture hall, and special exhibition galleries. These pleasant facilities are open to designers, students, and researchers working on theatrical productions. The new Centre draws on the costume and textile resources of the parent museum and also has its own collection of reference materials.

Publication. The Museum of Costume publishes a "Guide & Commentary" to the collection by Doris Langley Moore (38 pages). It is filled with interesting notes on both the fabrics and the fashions.

RIGHT. Detail of a brocaded-silk-damask dinner dress, c. 1860, with net lace sleeves. *Ulster Museum — 7–1951.*

FAR, RIGHT. The 17th Century Dungiven costume for a man. *Ulster Museum.*

BEDFORD

The Cecil Higgins Art Gallery
Castle Close
TEL: (0234) 53791

Halina Grubert, Curator

This is primarily a collection of costume and lace. Most of the pieces date from the late 19th or early 20th Century.

The costume collection numbers under a thousand pieces and the largest group (674 pieces) illustrates the wardrobe of middle-class women during the Victorian era — both the clothes they wore and the accessories they carried. A smaller group (65 pieces) covers the fashionable male wardrobe of the same period. Children's costume is shown in about 180 garments and accessories.

The lace collection contains some 400 pieces, with the emphasis on English lace from Bedfordshire, Buckinghamshire, Honiton, and Devon. It has a smaller group of 19th-Century laces from France, Italy, Belgium, Ireland, and Brazil, as well as a number of Renaissance pieces, some lace pattern books, and examples of modern machine lace.

There are about 80 pieces of embroidery in the collection, dating from the 18th and 19th Centuries, as well as a few quilts and other household linens.

BELFAST

Richard Atkinson & Co., Ltd.
Donegal Rd. BT12 6HT
TEL: Belfast 28079

David Nicholson, Director

The Atkinson firm has been manufacturing Irish poplin since 1820, and it maintains a small archive of selected fabrics produced by the company since its beginnings. Mr. Nicholson assures me that in normal times these historic examples of poplin would be made available to researchers. At the time of this writing (1974) conditions in Northern Ireland were not normal, and the archives were not accessible.

Irish poplin is constructed with a silk warp and a fine, worsted weft. It is known today for its use in men's ties — chiefly regimental stripes of great variety. In earlier times, however, the fabric was widely used for fancy waistcoats and women's gowns, often in floral designs. One such design, using gold thread, was woven for a court train worn by Queen Elizabeth. This and other early designs, as well as the wide range of woven stripings, are preserved in the company archives.

BELFAST

Ulster Museum
Botanic Gardens BT9 5AB
TEL: (0232) 668 2515

Elizabeth McCrum, Costume Asst.

The Ulster Museum (not to be confused with the Ulster Folk Museum at Holywood)

Back of a 17th Century woman's jacket with silk embroidery. *Ulster Museum.*

is now housed in a new building on the grounds of Belfast's Botanic Gardens. It is the National Museum of Northern Ireland and has a textile/costume collection of about 2,000 pieces.

The costume group is the larger, with about 1,600 garments and accessories for women, children, and men, dating from the 17th through the 19th Centuries. There are four dresses of Spitalfields silk, several gowns of 19th-Century brocaded silk, and a number of 19th-Century printed shawls.

Perhaps the most important piece in the collection is an early 17th-Century Irish man's costume found in an excavation near Dungiven, County Derry. It consists of tartan trews, a wool jacket, and a wool cape. The original costume is kept in storage, but the museum has a replica which it displays.

The museum also has ten garments from the Arctic, some with beaded decorations.

Among the flat textiles in the collection are the following Irish and English pieces: 43 samplers; 24 embroidered pictures in silk and in wool; 30 bed covers — quilted, printed, patchwork, knitted, and embroidered; about 75 examples of printed textiles dating from the 15th to the 19th Century; linen damasks from the 17th to the 19th Century; and 30 examples of English embroidery.

Among the pieces from other countries are about 70 woven and/or embroidered textiles from Europe, the Near East, India, and Africa. The most important group is from China, with about 100 pieces, including silk robes and embroidered panels.

There is a lace collection with about 170 pieces of Irish, English, and European origin, and seven tapestries, one from the workshop of Joshua Morris, dated 1725.

Publications. ''Women's Clothing of the 19th Century'' by Anne Wilson.
''The Dungiven Costume'' by Audrey Henshall & Wilfred Seaby.

English embroidered cushion top, early 17th Century. Wool and silk on canvas in Florentine and tent stitches. Given by Mrs. Longman.
Fitzwilliam — FMS 259 (T.132–1938).

BLACKBURN

Lewis Textile Museum
Exchange St. BB1 7AJ
TEL: Blackburn 59511

This museum exhibits textile machinery. It holds no collection of fabrics, but it deserves mention in this review, since it shows the breakthrough inventions of the 18th Century which laid the foundation for modern textile production. These inventions were all developed by men who lived and worked in or near Blackburn.

John Kay of Bury invented the flying shuttle in 1733. His son, Robert Kay, invented a drop box for the hand loom in 1760. James Hargreaves of Blackburn (Stanhill) invented the spinning jenny in 1764. Richard Arkwright of Preston invented the water frame for spinning in 1770. And Samuel Crompton of Bolton invented the spinning mule in 1779.

Replicas of these machines are shown in the museum (donated by T. B. Lewis). Also displayed are early domestic spinning and weaving equipment, as well as a 19th-Century Lancashire power loom. Designers and students can therefore see firsthand how textile machinery evolved from its domestic origins and transformed Lancashire from a rural province into one of the world's great industrial centers.

Publication. "Handbook of the Lewis Textile Museum" by W. Wilkinson and John S. Dimelor (20 pages with illustrations of machines). Contains a careful description of the inventions, the history of their development, and biographical notes on the inventors.

BOLTON

Museum & Art Gallery
Civic Centre BL1 1SE
TEL: Bolton 22311 (Ext. 357)
Angela Thomas, Keeper, Archaeology

The Bolton Museum holds at least two large groups of textiles which will be of interest to textile designers and students. They come from opposite ends of the time scale. One group is from ancient Egypt and numbers over 900 pieces. The other comes from Lancashire and includes some 200 pattern books from local mills, containing fabric samples of the 19th and 20th Centuries.

Details of these two major holdings follow.

The Egyptian collection is divided into four chronological groups:

1. Pre-Dynastic. There are 130 pieces in this category. They consist chiefly of linen fabrics found at archaeological sites in Mostagedda, Badari, and Gerzeh. They are plain fabrics in the main, dated at or before 5000 B.C., thus making them among the most ancient fabrics held by any museum.

2. Dynastic. About 160 pieces from the Dynastic period. Again, these are chiefly plain linens. Some were found at Tarkhan and date from the Old Kingdom (5500–4000 B.C.). Others are from Tell-el-Amarna and date from the second millennium B.C.

Spinning jenny (Hargreaves' design) from Bankfield Museum, Halifax, is similar to one at Lewis Textile Museum.

3. Graeco-Roman. About 75 specimens, some with tapestry decorations, others plainwoven or plaited. They come from Tanis and Fayum. Most date from a century or more before the Christian Era. One rare piece — a block-printed linen — is more recent and dates from the 2nd Century A.D.

4. Roman-Coptic. This is the largest group in the collection of ancient fabrics and one of the largest of this type and period held by any museum in the U.K. It consists of 540 pieces. Some were found at the archaeological site of Karanis. These are made of wool, linen, and goat's hair. Most are patterned fabrics. Also from the same site comes a skein of dyed cotton.

Other pieces in this large grouping are Coptic tapestry weaves from Armant, Fayum, and Tanis, dating from the 2nd to the 5th Century A.D.

Lancashire Cottons. The other major category in the Bolton Museum holdings consists of about 200 sample books from Lancashire mills, which have long been world-renowned for the quality of their woven cotton fabrics, especially men's shirtings.

Swatched in the sample books are an estimated 10,000 examples, mostly of woven cottons made during the 19th and early 20th Centuries. Since archives of this kind are hard (or impossible) to find in the U. K. today, the Bolton collection is a rare and important one. Moreover, the museum also holds a number of documents relating to the early textile industry in Lancashire.

In addition to these two major collections, Bolton also owns two smaller groups of textiles.

1. From Palestine. About 20 pieces, including a few fragments of very ancient linen found at Bethpelet, dating from about 1600 B.C., and some examples of Byzantine cloth.

2. From Peru. About 20 pieces of patterned fabric from the pre-Inca period.

Architect's elevation drawing of the classic Fitzwilliam Museum facade.

Among them are two early embroidered textiles in the Paracas style.

Bolton also owns a small collection of English costume, chiefly of the 19th and early 20th Centuries. There are about 50 dresses and a larger group of accessories. Also from the same period comes a small group of samplers, shawls, and domestic needlework.

CAMBRIDGE

Fitzwilliam Museum
Trumpington St. CB2 1RB
TEL: Cambridge 50023

Robin Crighton, Keeper, Applied Arts
Jane Palmer, Textile Consultant

The Fitzwilliam is one of England's outstanding museums, with notable collections of paintings, prints, sculpture, and antiquities, housed in an elegant Greek Revival building. It also owns rich and very diversified collections in the applied arts ranging from Dynastic Egypt to Victorian England.

The Applied Arts Department holds most of the textiles in the museum. The collection is small but very choice, and the staff members are friendly, helpful, and knowledgeable about the holdings. In all, the Fitzwilliam has about 1,200 pieces, including over 100 Coptic fragments held by the Antiquities Department.

One modest-sized gallery is devoted to textiles, and there are changing exhibits displayed in glass-topped cases. There is also a small but select library of about 250 volumes on textile design and fabric-forming processes.

The most important groups in the collection are the following.

Samplers. This is the largest and most important category. There are 384 pieces. Of these, over 300 are English; the rest are from other countries. They cover a period of almost 300 years, from the 17th to the 19th Century. More than 130 of the English samplers date from the 17th Century.

English Textiles. There are 133 pieces in the group, mainly embroideries of the 16th through the 19th Century. There is also one 15th-Century fragment of Opus Anglicanum.

Middle East. A substantial group of about 130 pieces, including a distinguished collection of Turkish towels and fine 18th-Century embroidery from Bokhara.

European Textiles. This group of about 75 textiles includes woven fabrics and tapestries from Belgium, France, Italy, Spain, and Norway. The earliest piece is a 15th-Century Flemish tapestry.

Greek Islands. An important collection of Greek Island embroidery, with 64 examples from different regions.

Lace. The lace group has about 60 pieces, representing both needle and bobbin laces from England and the continent.

Far East. There are 53 textiles from China, Japan, India, and Persia (Iran). Among them are a fine silk tapestry panel (K'o-ssu)

English lace-sampler detail, 17th Century. *Fitzwilliam — FMK 1636 (T.91–1928).*

from 15th-Century China and two excellent embroideries from Isfahan.

Carpets. A large group of 150 pieces. Fifty are on display in the museum galleries. The rest are kept in storage but can be seen by appointment. About 30 small rugs and saddlebags are part of the group.

Ancient Egypt. More than 100 fragments of Coptic tapestry work are held by the Antiquities Department of the museum.

CAMBRIDGE

University Museum of Archaeology & Ethnology
Downing St. CB2 3DZ
TEL: Cambridge 59714

Janice Stargardt, Keeper, S. E. Asia

I was surprised and impressed by the number of textiles on exhibit in this small but most interesting museum of ethnography. It is part of the Cambridge University complex and open to the public only from 2 to 4 P.M. Monday through Saturday. This limitation should not be allowed to discourage visitors. The museum is only a short walk from the Fitzwilliam and a two-hour survey of its collection would be a stimulating experience for any textile designer.

The exhibits are intelligently arranged for study, since this is a university collection and geared to the needs of students. Most displays carry informative captions which give the nonspecialist a good deal of insight into the cultures that produced the artifacts on display.

I would estimate that close to 1,000 textiles are exhibited behind glass in the pleasant galleries. The two strongest groups are from Southeast Asia and Peru. Following are some of the highlights.

Peru. One large, standing case with hinged panels contains 82 pieces of ancient

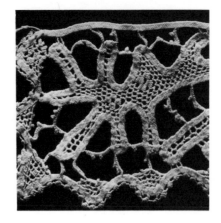

FAR LEFT. Rotunda and main entrance to the National Museum of Ireland.

LEFT. Magnified detail of Borris Point lace, one of many examples. *National Museum of Ireland — 298–1914.*

CAMBRIDGE UNIVERSITY MUSEUM Cont'd

Peruvian textile work, some of them among the best pieces held by any museum in the U. K. There are examples of both woven and painted textiles covering a long time span. The earliest pieces were found at the Paracas necropolis and date from the first millennium B.C. Other pieces are later in date and represent the cultures of Chancay, Ica, Nazca, and Tiahuanaca.

Elsewhere in the museum is a magnificent feather cape from the Chimu culture — 1200–1450 A.D.

Southeast Asia. The museum's holdings from this large area are considered to be the strongest in the British Isles, and the textiles on exhibit represent many different regions and cultures. As inspiration for contemporary textile design I was particularly attracted to the following.

1. Feather cloaks from the Sandwich Islands and from Hawaii.

2. A large and impressive exhibit of tapa-cloth patterns, including clear descriptions and illustrations of the cloth-making process, as well as the colorings used — soot and red clay.

3. Fine examples of batikwork from Java and Bali.

4. Cotton pillow covers of dramatic design from Borneo.

5. A number of exotic weavings from northeast Thailand.

6. Silk mats with ikatlike patterning made in Borneo.

7. A most interesting group of woven stripings from Sarawak.

8. An impressive painted tanka (banner) from Tibet.

9. An exceptional group of blankets and body cloths from Assam.

10. Central America is also represented in the collection by a large exhibit of blankets and ethnic costumes from Guatemala and Mexico.

CARDIFF

Welsh Folk Museum
St. Fagans
TEL: Cardiff 561357

This museum is a branch of the National Museum of Wales, located at St. Fagans, near Cardiff. Among the exhibits of Welsh folkways is the Esgair Moel Woollen Factory, which has been transplanted from Llanwrtyd in Breconshire. It dates from 1760 and illustrates a typical Welsh textile mill operated by a water wheel. Carding, spinning, weaving, fulling, and dyeing are demonstrated on this early equipment, which produces fabrics, bed covers, and rugs in traditional Welsh patterns. They are for sale at the museum.

DUBLIN

National Museum of Ireland
Kildare St., Dublin 2
TEL: Dublin 65521

John Teahan, Keeper, Art Division
Oliver Snoddy, Asst. Keeper

The National Museum of Ireland holds an important collection of lace, as well as a small but interesting collection of woven, embroidered, and printed fabrics.

Facilities for research are minimal, and there is currently (1974) no curator for the textile collection. Fortunately for researchers, however, most of the best pieces in the collection are on open display in the museum galleries.

The main textile exhibit is housed in Gallery 15, off the upper balcony which surrounds the large, glass-roofed central hall. In addition, the walls of a large section in the same upper balcony (Gallery 12) are handsomely covered with many framed examples of very fine laces, representing every type made in Ireland as well as pieces from the most important centers of European lacemaking. They cover a time span from the early 17th Century to the recent past.

In Gallery 12 there are excellent examples of appliqué and guipure lace from Carrickmacross; tambour and runwork from Limerick. Needlepoint lace is shown is pieces from Youghal, Kenmare, New Ross, Tynan, and Inishmacsaint. Crochet and point d'Irlande pieces from Cork and Clones are also on exhibit, as well as examples of tatting made in Ardee and Ballintubber.

The Textile Room itself (Gallery 15) holds a small, compact, but surprisingly representative collection of woven, embroidered, and printed fabrics from many of the important periods and cultures in the history of textile design. These are exhibited either on hinged panel frames or under glass in standing cases which are covered with easily removable opaque blinds to protect them from fading.

Among the pieces displayed are the following.

Egypt. A substantial group of Coptic fragments (61 pieces) are shown on hinged panels. There are excellent examples of wool tapestry work from the 6th to the 10th Century in a fine state of preservation.

Peru. Similar panels display 26 examples of pre-Columbian weaving and embroidery from Peru, dating from 400–1400 A.D.

Samplers. Eleven examples of Irish, English, and Italian work.

Embroidery. Representative pieces of 18th- and 19th-Century embroidery from Ireland, England, China, France, Spain, Portugal, Persia, Turkey, and the Greek Islands. Also several fine examples of Irish and English stumpwork.

Weaving. A few brocaded silks and velvets from Italy, dating from the 15th to the 16th Century, and Irish damasks, dating from as early as 1734.

RIGHT. Venetian grospoint lace, 1650. *National Museum of Ireland — 15(21–1878).*

FAR RIGHT. Carrickmacross lace, appliqué, and guipure, 1912. *National Museum of Ireland.*

Patchwork. Irish patchwork quilts of the 19th Century.

Prints. A small group of printed textiles, including French toiles. Perhaps the most outstanding piece on display is a large repeat of the famous "Volunteer Furniture" print based on the provincial military review held in Dublin's Phoenix Park on June 4, 1782. It is a copperplate print by Harpur & Cunningham of Leixlip, made for Edward Clarke's Irish Furniture Warehouse in 1783. (Incidentally, the world's first textiles printed from copperplates are now believed to have been made at the Drumcondra printworks, outside Dublin, in 1752. The process was not used in England until 1756.)

Other walls in the museum exhibit Chinese and Japanese tapestries, a William Morris "Flora" tapestry by Burne-Jones and H. Dearle, a number of embroidered pieces from the first half of the 18th Century, and several Flemish high-mass vestments of the late 15th Century in brocaded velvet and cloth of gold.

The museum has a small costume exhibit (Gallery 13) with examples of changing fashions from the years 1750, 1810, 1840, and 1870.

Publication. "Guide to the Collection of Lace." by Ada K. Longfield, 1970 (46 pages with 22 excellent B/W photographs showing different types of lace). European lacemaking is reviewed from its early beginnings, and the history of Irish lace is told in detail.

Photographs. The museum library has several hundred glass negatives of pieces in the textile collection, most of them showing laces.

DUNDEE

The Scottish Tartans Society
Broughty Castle Museum DD5 2BE
TEL: (0382) 76121

The most extensive and the best documented collection of Scottish tartans in existence is held by the Scottish Tartans Society in the Broughty Castle Museum.

Over 1,200 tartan specimens are cataloged in the collection, and almost all are well documented. An elaborate filing system provides all available information on each specimen, including origins of names and social history.

The Society's holdings now includes the McGregor Hastie Collection of some 900 tartans, together with notes on each and correspondence built up over 30 years.

A comprehensive library attached to the collection covers all facets of Highland tartan dress. It contains about 2,000 letters from Wilsons of Bannockburn, one of the first companies to manufacture tartans on a large scale in the early 19th Century.

The Society is a leading resource for the most authoritative current books on the tartans and the clans of Scotland. (List sent on request.) A clan map of the Scottish Highlands is also available.

The Invermark District Check, as shown in the E.S. Harrison book *Our Scottish District Checks.*

DURHAM

Gulbenkian Museum of Oriental Art
University of Durham
Elvet Hill DH1 3TH
TEL: (0385) 66711

Philip S. Rawson, Curator

The Gulbenkian Museum holds a small but quite specialized collection of Far Eastern art fabrics, which serves as a resource for the School of Oriental Studies.

There are about 160 pieces in the collection, and more than half of them are Chinese in origin. These include Mandarin and ceremonial robes, other decorative garments, a number of art embroideries, tapestries, shawls, and a large 12-part screen.

Other Eastern cultures represented in the collection are India, Burma, Japan, and Iraq. Among these pieces are shawls and saris, cushion covers, side bags, head scarves, and wall hangings, most of them worked with art embroidery.

EDINBURGH

"Our Scotish District Checks"
by E. S. Harrison (1968)

The National Association of
Scottish Woollen Manufacturers
8 Wemyss Pl. EH3 6EQ
TEL: (031) 225-4904

I looked long and diligently in the United Kingdom for a substantial collection of Scottish District Checks which I could list and review in this volume. I did so out of the conviction that these anonymous patterns rank with the world's most important textile designs.

But no such collection was to be found in any museum. I may have stirred up something in my search, for I detected a spark in several curatorial eyes. Perhaps,

The Arndilly pattern shown in the book *Our Scottish District Checks*. It was introduced before 1870. Its colors on off-white ground are: black, greenish fawn, reddish fawn, peacock, reseda.

SCOTTISH DISTRICT CHECKS Cont'd

eventually, at least one Scottish museum will own a study collection of these ubiquitous textiles (see note at end of this review).

Lacking a collection, I have resorted to reviewing a book as the only current source of authoritative information on the subject. The book is listed above.

Mr. Harrison was not a writer by profession. He was a mill owner, the head of James Johnston & Co. of Elgin, in the north of Scotland. His mill was among the first to produce District Checks in the middle of the 19th Century, and it had a world-wide reputation for the quality of its luxurious cashmere, vicuña, and wool fabrics.

In 1931 Mr. Harrison began to write a series of anonymous essays on Scottish fabrics. They were handsomely printed and issued as pamphlets by the National Association of Scottish Woollen Manufacturers in Edinburgh. The rare quality of the prose and the handsome format earned them an international circulation in the trade. So much so that in 1956 they were reissued in one volume under the title "Scottish Woollens." I own and treasure a copy of this book. It is filled with a contagious love of the Scottish countryside, and it is written in a rambling style so beguiling and so elegantly phrased that it bears comparison with the best of 19th-Century British belles lettres.

I met Mr. Harrison in 1962. More out of literary curiosity than research into textiles, I traveled from New York to the Johnston mill in Elgin. I wanted to meet the man who could write such lucid prose while at the same time operating a successful textile mill.

The man I met was small, spare, and retiring. Though he must at that time have been close to 75, he was sprightly and full of wit. Age had not diminished his ener-

gies. Though he did not mention it, he must then have been engaged in the herculean task of assembling the research for the book on District Checks. What I remember most about that visit was his reaction to my praise of his writing. "Oh," he said, looking at me sharply with his bright blue eyes, "I always patterned myself on Walter Pater."

The book on District Checks stems from two of the earlier essays written in 1933. But the material has been vastly expanded.

What does the book contain?

Exactly 106 different District Check designs, all reproduced in full color and in full scale. The reproduction is sharp and clear so that in almost all cases — as Mr. Harrison points out — "Any weaver can count the threads." All patterns reproduced in the book were especially woven for that purpose.

Each design is accompanied by an extensive note which describes the technical construction of the pattern and gives its origin, together with much fascinating information on its background and use.

The Russell Glenurquhart District Check is colored in brown, moss, russet, and wine. *Our Scottish District Checks.*

The reproductions and pattern descriptions run to 123 pages. They are introduced by a 25-page historical essay written in a charming and discursive style, similar to that of the collected essays. From this introduction I learned the following facts.

1. District Checks were introduced in the 1830s and were first so named by Mr. Harrison's father, George Harrison, a tweed merchant in Edinburgh.

2. They were developed as designs to be used by the newer Scottish landowners to clothe and identify their retainers. This distinguished them from the tartans, which were identifying symbols of the much more ancient Scottish clans. Mr. Harrison's definition reads: "A check or design must belong to a particular estate and must have been used to clothe the owners and their staff."

3. Most District Checks are based on the traditional black-and-white shepherd check — literally worn by shepherds in the field.

4. The colors used were generally conceived as protective coloring, blending into the Scottish landscape. As such, the fabrics were chiefly used for hunting clothes.

5. Technical specifications. The original fabrics were heavy — 24 ounces to the 58-inch yard. The weave was mostly a common twill — two over and two under each warp thread. The yarns were two-ply cheviot quality and 24-cut on the Galashiels system. The cloth count was more or less 26 threads to the inch in both directions — "square" cloths. They were thoroughly milled, or felted, to give protection against the Scottish weather.

6. Johnstons of Elgin and Ballantyne of Walkerburn were the two mills responsible for weaving most of the District Checks adopted by Scottish estates from about the year 1850 onwards.

Note. As of late 1974, the 106 District Check sample pieces (woven to be

RIGHT. Shawl pattern No. 6071, probably Paisley, 1840–55. *National Museum of Antiquities of Scotland — TRA–11.*

FAR RIGHT. Pattern No. 5069, probably Paisley, 1840–55. Same source as above.

photographed for the book) were all stored at the printers — Pillans & Wilson, 20 Bernard Terrace, Edinburgh EH8 9NY. Tel: (031) 667-2036. A commercial printing house is not a public museum, but perhaps the samples could be examined there if application were made through the National Association of Scottish Woollen Manufacturers. My hope is that the Association will eventually donate the collection to a Scottish museum.

EDINBURGH

National Museum of Antiquities of Scotland   Queen St. EH2 1JD
TEL: (031) 556-8921

Helen Bennett, Research Asst.

The National Museum of Antiquities owns several treasures of unusual interest to textile designers and students.

The most important of these are three large pattern books from the Leven Printfield, dated 1792–1804. The Vale of Leven (river Leven) is just south of Loch Lomond. It was justly famous for the quality and design of textile prints produced there by three firms during the last quarter of the 18th Century.

Students of early print design should be interested in two expertly researched articles on "Scottish 18th-Century Chintz" by Francina Irwin in the Burlington Magazine for September and October, 1965. The pattern books noted above are carefully described in the second of these articles.

One of the pattern books contains designs for printed shawls. They are done in ink and watercolor and were the originals from which wood blocks were made for printing. Francina Irwin points out that Edinburgh was a center for the Scottish shawl industry before Paisley came into the picture in the early part of the 19th Century. This sample book documents that fact. There are about 70 designs in the book.

A second book contains original designs for apparel and home-furnishings fabrics printed in the late 18th Century.

The third volume is a factory record of impressions made from wood blocks used to print both shawls and fabric yardage.

In addition to these three treasures, the museum also holds three pattern books for Paisley shawls, as well as another of Paisley pattern proofs dating from 1840–55. There are also ten wood blocks with designs similar to those shown in the books.

Design for printed shawl from Leven Printfield Pattern Books, end of 18th Century. Same source as above.

Among other holdings in the museum collections are:

Paisley Shawls. About 30 shawls in a variety of designs.

Blankets. About 40 examples of traditional Scottish blankets and Arisaids. The Arisaid was a large, woven, wool fabric, similar to a blanket but also used by women as a shawl. Some of them have checked patterns on a white ground.

Tartans. About 300 examples of early wool tartans. Most are in sample books, but the samples are large enough to show pattern repeats, and a number are named and dated. They illustrate both the "soft" wool constructions and the "hard" worsted types. The earliest piece in the group is a "hard" tartan of wool and silk. It is a large piece (26 x 73) and is said to have been woven in the 17th Century by the Macphersons of Crubin.

Linens. About 80 pieces of damask tablecloths and napkins, from 1700–1856.

Archaeological. Some 45 fragments and complete garments found in Scotland during archaeological explorations. They date from prehistoric times to 1700 and are chiefly locally made woolen textiles.

Costume. The largest unit in the museum's textile collection consists of several thousand garments and accessories worn in Scotland from 1750 to the present.

Facilities for display and research are currently inadequate at the museum, since the collections have outgrown the present building, and many of the textiles are stored outside the museum. Plans for a new building are under consideration, and they include research facilities. Nevertheless, the museum is actively engaged in collecting Scottish textiles and expects to add Scottish District Checks to its holdings in the near future. Meanwhile the collection of pattern books, tartans, and other pieces can be seen and studied by appointment.

FAR LEFT. Middle Eastern panel in cotton and linen, combining Turkish embroidery, Greek or Dalmation lace, and Persian tent stitch. 18th to 19th Century. *Royal Scottish Museum — 1962.1199.*

LEFT. Algerian scarf, 18th Century. Linen embroidered with silk. *Royal Scottish Museum — 1962–1242.*

EDINBURGH

Royal Scottish Museum
Art & Archaeology Department
Chambers St. EH1 1JF
TEL: (031) 225-7534

Revel Oddy, Asst. Keeper
Dale Idiens, Asst. Keeper

The approach to the Royal Scottish Museum is somewhat less than inviting. The long building facade of blackened stone is dour and a little forbidding. But an unexpected pleasure awaits you as you enter the building and find yourself in a different world. You stand in a great, light-filled hall, more than a hundred feet long and rising three stories on slender iron pillars to a web of iron Gothic arches which support a vast, skylit roof. It is a magnificent piece of space, echoing the splendor of the fabled Crystal Palace, after which it was modeled in 1861.

The great hall is surrounded by two long galleries, and on the first of these is displayed a representative collection of the museum's textile/costume holdings in more than a hundred standing cases.

It is a rich and impressive collection, very diversified and numbering some 8,000 pieces. Of this total, about 5,000 are flat textiles; over 3,000 are costumes and accessories. All are held by the museum's Department of Art & Archaeology.

The collection is divided into three main sections.

1. European. There are approximately 5,000 pieces in this section, about equally divided between flat textiles and costume.

2. Asiatic. About 1,300 textiles and 650 costumes.

3. "Primitive." This is a smaller group of slightly more than 300 pieces.

In addition, the museum owns about 150 pieces from ancient Egypt, a similar number from ancient Peru, a small group of 32 pieces representing American Plains Indians, and over 200 large sample books of Scottish textile prints.

Highlights from these different categories are outlined below.

Needlework. One of the strongest and most important segments in the collection consists of embroideries. Most of them were presented to the museum by the Needlework Development Scheme and are described in a 1965 catalog published by the museum.

European embroideries dominate the group, with a very varied collection of colored work, white work, samplers, bedspreads, patchwork quilts, pictures,

Main Hall of the Royal Scottish Museum before a white marble floor was laid.

panels, hangings, and chair seats. The following countries are represented: Albania, Algeria, Armenia, Austria, Belgium, the British Isles, Bulgaria, the Canary Islands, China, Czechoslovakia, Egypt, Estonia, Finland, Denmark, France, Germany, the Greek Islands, Hungary, India, Ireland, Italy, Mexico, Morocco, Norway, Palestine, the Phillipines, Poland, Portugal, Sicily, Spain, Sweden, Switzerland, Syria, Turkey, the United States, Yemen, Yugoslavia, and Zanzibar.

Lace. This is a major collection of some 800 pieces, with wide representation from many countries and dating from the 16th Century forward. It includes some rare examples of Bebilla lace and stumpwork. The main sources of the work are: Africa (East), Belgium, Czechoslovakia, France, Germany, the Greek Islands, Holland, Ireland, Italy, Malta, Mexico, Portugal, Scotland, South America, Spain, Sweden, Turkey, and the U.S.S.R.

Woven Textiles. This group consists of brocades, brocatelles, damasks, and similar decorated pieces in the form of panels, borders, and fragments. The earliest textile dates from the 14th Century. There are some 160 pieces in the group, chiefly from Britain, France, Italy, Poland, Spain, Switzerland, Turkey, and the U.S.S.R. Included here are a number of fine Paisley shawls.

Printed Textiles. Close to 200 pieces, showing representative work from European countries and covering a long time span.

Tapestries. A small collection, including some 17th and 18th Century pieces as well as modern works by contemporary artist-weavers in Scotland.

Costume. This is a major collection of some 2,400 garments and accessories, chiefly from the British Isles. The earliest outfit is from the mid–17th Century. The most recent is contemporary.

RIGHT. Woven white silk gauze shawl with printed stripes, French or German, 1850–1900. Gift of Miss F. C. Campbell. *Royal Scottish Museum — 1969–21.*

FAR RIGHT. Embroidered white cotton tablecloth, Portuguese, 1835–40. From Needlework Development Scheme. *Royal Scottish Museum — 1962.1221.*

Asia. The museum holds some 2,000 pieces, representing work from different Asiatic countries and dating from the 10th Century to modern times.

From *China* there are about 300 pieces, including a large number of court robes (120) and a fine group of silk tapestries.

From *Japan* there are also about 300 pieces, mainly fragments mounted on study cards. They include 18th- and 19th-Century brocades and satin embroideries.

From *India* there are some 200 pieces, including large painted-and-dyed palampores, Kashmir shawls, and many intricate embroideries.

From *Persia* there are about 250 pieces, including Nakshe embroideries, brocades, and block-printed textiles.

Smaller groupings of fabrics represent work from Malaya, Baluchistan, Djakarta (batiks), Bhutan, and Burma.

"Primitive". The misnamed "primitive" collection is not large in numbers (about 315 pieces), but it represents work from many different cultures in the Pacific and in Africa. Most of them date from the second half of the 19th Century.

Tapa cloths are a major grouping (187 pieces) in this category — chiefly from the island countries of Polynesia and Melanesia.

Another group includes some 60 pieces of batik and tapa cloth from Indonesia.

Africa — West and North — is represented by about 65 pieces of resist-dyed cotton, as well as embroideries and robes.

Ancient Egypt. Two main groups of very early textiles are included in this category.

1. Graeco-Roman fabrics from Egyptian burying grounds, dating from the 3rd to the 6th Century A.D. About 65 pieces.

2. Coptic tapestry-woven fragments, dating from the 4th to 8th Century A.D. About 85 pieces.

Ancient Peru. Among the 137 pieces in this fine collection are the most ancient textiles owned by the museum. They are from Paracas and are dated at 2500 B.C. or earlier. The group also contains Nazca textiles from the 1st to the 6th Century A.D. and more recent pieces from the 14th to the 16th Century. The collection includes garments, bags, and patterned fragments.

U.S. Plains Indians. The thirty-odd pieces in this group date from the middle to the end of the 19th Century and chiefly represent Indian decorations on cloth acquired from Europeans.

Sample Books. Perhaps the rarest and most interesting holding at the Royal Scottish Museum is a collection of some 200 sample books covering about 100 years — from the 1830s to the 1930s. These books are pattern records of the United Turkey Red Company, textile printers operating in Alexandria, near Glasgow.

The reason these sample books are so interesting is that they represent one of the few records we have of a large cotton-printing industry which flourished in Scotland from the middle of the 18th Century onward.

In 1785 this industry adopted a new color — Turkey Red — which became its hallmark for more than 100 years. It was a bright red, fast in color, and derived from the madder plant. It was first developed in France around 1750. A vast range of patterns was printed on these Turkey-Red grounds, including bandanna hankerchiefs. Beginning toward the end of the 18th Century, these printed cottons were the mainstay of a major export trade moving from Scottish printfields to distant markets — particularly to India and the West Indies.

Here is proof, then, that the old Scottish adage of "carrying coals to Newcastle" was reversed. And the designs were not Scottish designs. They were made specifically for the tastes of foreign markets, much bolder and more colorful than would have been acceptable in the home market. In that lies their chief interest for contemporary designers.

According to Margaret H. Swain — who investigated this area of the collection in depth — the museum also holds several hundred additional print designs of a similar nature, which came to the Royal Scottish in 1857 as a bequest from the J. Pender firm, textile printers who operated in Glasgow and Manchester. This group of patterns reveals the types of cotton prints made in Scotland for export to such foreign markets as the United States, Argentina, Turkey, Persia, Italy, the Cape of Good Hope, China, Java, and the East Indies.

These documents make a fascinating record, still largely unexplored.

GLASGOW

Art Gallery & Museum

Kelvingrove Park G3 8 AG
TEL: (041) 334-1134

Brian J.R. Blench, Keeper, Dec. Arts

For those who think of Glasgow as a dense industrial city, the area around its Art Gallery & Museum will come as a pleasant surprise. Kelvingrove Park is a quiet region of fine old houses and rolling parkland on a hill overlooking central Glasgow. The museum itself is housed in a huge and impressive red sandstone structure with a great skylit exhibition hall.

Unfortunately most of the museum's textile collection is at present inaccessible to researchers, since it will eventually be housed in a different building devoted entirely to costume and textiles. By the end of 1975 or early 1976, it will be moved to Aikenhead House, an 1810 mansion in King's Park. By then, the costume/textile collection will have been recataloged, and full research

Model of a projected new museum for the Burrell Collection to be located in Pollok Park on the South Side of Glasgow. Design by Barry Gasson and John Meunier.

facilities, including a textile study room and library, will be available. Future exhibits will be designed to reflect both social trends and technological development.

At present, the collection of flat fabrics is small, though the costume collection is extensive — over 3,000 pieces. The emphasis is on 18th- and 19th-Century garments worn in Scotland and England.

Flat textiles held by the Decorative Arts department number only about 200 pieces, ranging from 15th-Century Italian damasks to 19th-Century ecclesiastical vestments. However, the department is now actively engaged in collecting contemporary Scottish textiles and expects to specilize in this area when the collection moves into its new home.

In the meantime, the museum's costume/textile exhibits include the following: children's clothing from 1860–90; men's embroidered waistcoats from 1760–1850; and women's dresses from 1770–1911, the 1920s, and the 1930s.

A small number of textiles are exhibited in the museum's ethnography galleries. They include pieces from Central and North Africa, beadwork of the American Indians, and a few other American Indian textiles from the Northwest coast and Northeast Canada.

GLASGOW

The Burrell Collection
Camphill Museum
Queen's Park G41 2EW
TEL: (041) 632-1350

William Wells, Keeper

The Burrell Collection is a unit of the Glasgow Museums & Art Galleries and currently occupies a large mansion in Queen's Park. However, a new and very advanced structure has been designed to house the collection, and a model is on display at the Camphill Museum. It was originally scheduled to be completed by 1978 on a handsome woodland site in Pollok Park on the south side of Glasgow. Because of inflated building costs, this plan has now been held up. When and if completed, the new structure will contain a textile study room and will become a most elegant modern home for this outstanding art collection of some 8,000 pieces, given to the city by Sir William Burrell in 1944. Its holdings include world-renowned Gothic treasures and a fine group of 19th-Century French paintings, as well as silver, porcelain, furniture, stained glass, carpets, tapestries, and needlework.

The textile section of the holdings is not large in numbers (789 pieces, to be exact), but it is outstanding. The collection of medieval and Renaissance tapestries is considered to be among the most important in the world. The same is true of the museum's Persian and other Near Eastern carpets.

Coptic tapestry roundel, 9–10th Century. *Burrell Collection — Inv. 86.*

The Burrell Collection as a whole has been remarkably well organized and cataloged under the direction of its knowledgeable and helpful curator, William Wells. The present study room holds a comprehensive file of excellent photographs (both B/W prints and color slides) covering most pieces in the collections, and research is encouraged.

The textile holdings are broken down into three main divisions — tapstries, carpets, and needlework. Each division is described below.

Tapestries. A total of 213 pieces in six categories:

1. German and Swiss tapestries of the 14th, 15th, and 16th Centuries — 39 pieces. Of these, 10 are ascribed to south Germany, 3 to Middle Germany, 2 to Lower Rhineland, 5 to Middle Rhineland, 13 to Upper Rhineland, and 13 to Switzerland.

2. Franco-Burgundian tapestries of the late 14th, 15th, and 16th Centuries—106 pieces. Of these, 25 show hunting and outdoor scenes, 15 are devoted to myth and romance, 15 are of the millefleurs type, 30 have religious or allegorical scenes, and 16 are fragmentary.

3. Netherlands/France. Four 16th-Century tapestries woven in the Netherlands for English patrons and one early 18th-Century tapestry.

4. English/European — 38 pieces. They include English Sheldon valances, cushion covers, and other work of the 17th and 18th Centuries.

5. Coptic tapestry weavings — 18 fragments.

6. Peru — Eight fragments of pre-Conquest work and one post-Conquest hanging.

Carpets. A total of 122 carpets, prayer rugs, and fragments from the 16th, 17th, 18th, and 19th Centuries. Of these, 72 are from

Needlework panel, possibly English, early 17th Century. Satin ground with raised and padded motifs. *Burrell Collection — Inv. 58.*

Central Asia (chiefly Persia), 16 from the Caucasus, 10 from India, and 24 from Turkey. Among them are the famous 17th-Century "Wagner" garden carpet and the equally renowned 17th-Century Caucasian "Dragon" carpet.

Needlework. There are 452 pieces of embroidery and lace in the collection. They include:

1. English embroidery — 228 pieces. Of these, 15 are ecclesiastical vestments of the 14th, 15th, and 16th Centuries; 26 are panels of the 16 and 17th Centuries, worked with flowers and/or animals; 44 have Biblical subjects; and 38 deal with either mythical or pastoral themes. In addition, there are 24 costume accessories and 75 home-furnishing embroideries, 8 of them with ornamental raised work.

2. English samplers of the 16th, 17th, and 18th Centuries — 26 pieces.

3. Embroidered bed covers, chiefly from Bokhara — 19 pieces.

4. Jacobean curtains with crewelwork — 59 pairs.

5. Lace — 120 pieces from France, England, Flanders, and Spain.

It should be said that almost all the 789 pieces in the Burrell textile collection are of high quality, showing notably fine design work in each category and from each period.

Publications. A number of articles about the tapestries and carpets in the Burrell Collection have been published in contemporary art periodicals. The museum is able to supply a list of over 30 such monographs. It has also published a small picture book on the tapestries. Additional surveys of the textile holdings are contained in the illustrated annual reports which have been issued by the Glasgow Museums & Art Galleries from 1944 to date.

GLASGOW

Hunterian Museum
Glasgow University G12 8QQ
TEL: (041) 339-8855

Dr. Anne Robertson, Curator

The Hunterian Museum is part of Glasgow University and holds collections of fine arts, geology, archaeology, and ethnography.

Within the ethnography department there is a small group of textiles, but they are not readily available for study. For textile designers and students, the main interest will probably be a group of about 25 tapa cloths from the South sea islands. There is also some finger-woven cloth from New Zealand, and two pieces of feather work from Polynesia.

HALIFAX

Bankfield Museum
Akroyd Park HX3 6HG
TEL: Elland 2540

R. A. Innes, Director
Mrs. M. Pitman, Keeper, Textiles

The Bankfield Museum comes as a surprise. In a provincial, industrial city like Halifax you do not expect to find a textile collection of such size, range, and historic scope. Its textile holdings are officially calculated to be in the area of 20,000 to 25,000 pieces. This would make it the second largest textile collection in the U. K. — next to the Victoria & Albert Museum.

I have examined the accession files, but I cannot vouch for the figure. I suspect it is somewhat overestimated, since no exact count has ever been taken. The official figure includes costumes and textile tools of all kinds, which, together, are far more numerous than the holdings of flat textiles. This is not said to diminish the importance of the collection. It is most impressive, with a wide range of art fabrics and ethnic costumes from different cultures and periods.

These holdings were acquired through the efforts of the museum's first curator, H. Ling Roth, who had friends among anthropologists working in several parts of the world and who persuaded them to collect textiles and costume, as well as primitive spinning and weaving equipment, for the museum. These acquisitions began in 1897 when the museum was founded. They have since been expanded by gifts from other donors.

The museum is unique on another level. The exhibits focus on technique as well as on design and history. Halifax was and continues to be a center of wool textile manufacturing, and the museum reflects the wool industry's concern with the techniques of forming fabrics. Thus, when the museum collected textiles, it tried always to collect the means of production as well — the tools and equipment for

English table spinning wheel, one of many such pieces in the Bankfield collection. *Bankfield Museum, Halifax.*

The Bankfield Museum, Halifax, an unexpected treasure house filled with textiles from many cultures and the tools that made them.

BANKFIELD MUSEUM
Cont'd

spinning, weaving, lacemaking, and knitting by both hand and machine.

The exhibits in the museum are rich in technical information. They are concerned to show and to explain how a specific textile is made as well as how it looks. Wherever possible, the tools are shown alongside the end product, and this gives the exhibits a dimension not usually found in art museums. Captions are always detailed and informative.

The Bankfield collection is therefore primarily a study collection, designed to stimulate and intrigue an inquiring mind. This approach is fortified by a fairly extensive textile reference library of both English and foreign texts. It is further extended by the fact that members of the curatorial staff understand and can duplicate many of the fabric-forming methods shown in the exhibits. In addition, most items in the collection are cataloged and cross-indexed by type and region of origin.

The exhibits tend to be somewhat old-fashioned and closely packed, but they are often well lighted, and this is more than can be said for most textile/costume exhibits in the U. K. The Bankfield galleries offer designers and students a rich and varied canvas of materials in standing cases, wall panels, and model rooms. Their appeal will probably be strongest to handweavers and other handcraft workers, but the industrial designer will also find much that is stimulating in the collection. A visit to Halifax is well worth the trip.

On the collections themselves, the following offers a generalized breakdown of the main holdings.

Great Britain. A wide range of British textile examples, including 15th-Century velvets, 17th Century linens and fustians, 18th-Century brocades and chintz, and 19th-Century Yorkshire menswear fabrics.

Embroideries include 15th-Century ecclesiastical work, Jacobean appliqué and 17th-Century stump- and crewelwork, and samplers from the 18th Century forward. Also held are costumes dating from the late 18th Century through the mid–20th Century, with a special range of baby clothes.

Western Europe. French 18th-Century brocades, French Aubusson tapestry work, Dutch 17th-Century linens, Mehlenburg peasant headdresses, Spanish farmers' costumes and textiles of wool and hemp, and Italian 17th-Century reticula work and brocades.

Balkans and Central Europe. Peasant costumes and embroideries collected before World War I. Catholic, Moslem, and Orthodox peoples are represented by national and racial groupings. Special emphasis is given to shirt embroideries from Albania, Bosnia, Dalmatia, Montenegro, Moravia, Serbia, and Slovakia. The collection also holds examples of decorated towels, bed linens, headdresses, and aprons from the same regions.

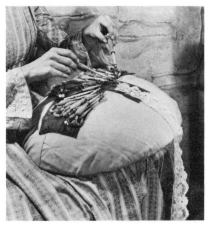

This exhibit of pillow lace making is one of many similar exhibits which fill the galleries of the Bankfield Museum.

Africa. Congo basin textiles, and ancient Egyptian and Coptic pieces found in tombs and dating from 200 to 900 A.D.

Far East. From Burma (Shan and Kachin tribes) come native fabrics and costumes, mostly of cotton and revealing the Chinese influence in decoration. This section also includes a large group of cotton shoulder bags with seed decorations. It is probably the best collection of Burmese textiles in the country.

From *India* come embroideries of different types, Kashmir shawls, and Madras "shadow" work.

From *Assam* (Naga tribes) comes a large group of cotton textiles and costumes.

From *China* there are embroideries of the 18th and 19th Centuries, as well as some costumes.

From *Japan* there are brocaded fabrics and embroidery.

From the *Fiji Islands* there are tapa cloths with painted designs.

From the *Americas* comes a small collection of Peruvian Inca textiles and a number of American Indian fabrics and moccasins.

Crossley Mosaics. This is a special group of textiles, unique to Bankfield and requiring some explanation.

In Halifax there is a firm of carpet manufacturers named John Crossley & Son. From 1850–1869 this company successfully produced and sold a wide range of small, wool picture carpets, which have come to be known as "Crossley Mosaics." They were produced by an ingenious patented technique.

The technique was invented by a German refugee technician named Schubert, who came to work for Crossley in the middle of the 19th Century. Essentially, it involved the reproduction of a design with the ends of worsted warp yarns.

Once a design was chosen (a painting, a

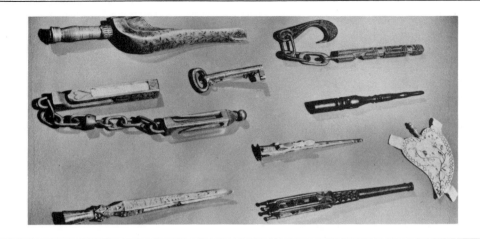

Carved wooden knitting sheaths from the Bankfield Museum collection. These sheaths were worn on the right hip to hold the work in progress.

figure, a scene, etc.), it was transferred to graph paper. The colors in each square of the graph paper were then simulated by different-colored warp yarns. These warp yarns were drawn through a long frame and arranged according to the pattern on the graph. The warp threads (exposed in cross-section at the end of the frame) showed the whole design — much as a design would appear on the end cross-section of a rock-candy roll, except that this was rectangular in shape.

A piece of linen the same size as the design was then glued to the warp-thread picture, and a slice (about 4 mm thick) was cut through the whole structure — the way a meat cutter slices bologna. This made a yarn picture on a linen backing. From one such frame about 900 pictures could be sliced. And if they were sliced from opposite ends of the frame, the pictures would be mirror images of one another.

By today's standards the subjects of these Crossley Mosaics might well fall into the category of "camp" art, but they were very popular in Victorian times, and the Bankfield Museum has a large collection of them. They were used for fire screens, wall pictures, table covers, small rugs, etc. They show romantic scenes, landscapes, floral decorations, and reproductions of paintings by popular artists of the day, such as Landseer.

Museum Exhibits

During my visit to the Bankfield Museum the largest gallery on the ground floor was devoted to an exhibit of Crossley Mosaics. There was also an extensive exhibit of uniforms and paraphernalia from a local infantry and cavalry regiment. These are not necessarily permanent exhibits, though they seemed of long duration.

The big second floor of the museum shows the major textile holdings, together with the tools and equipment used in making them. Listed below are some of the highlights.

Tartans & Checks. A large panel display shows about 60 examples of wool tartans and a smaller number of Scottish District Checks and Shetlands. To each sample is attached technical instructions for weaving the pattern. Weaving designers will find this exhibit especially rewarding.

Tapa Cloths. A number of different patterned tapa cloths from the Fiji Islands are shown, together with the wooden beaters used to make the cloth from the inner bark of palm trees. The technique is explained through simple and informative captions.

Eiderdown Bed Cover. A rare piece made from the breast down of the eider drake. Some 60 birds were used to make this small, beautiful cover. Happily, the practice is now prohibited by law.

Chilkat Blanket. A very good example of this typical textile is on exhibit, finger-woven by the Indians of southern Alaska.

Woven Textiles. Examples and explanations of brocade, tissue, damask, lampas, and Callimanco.

Replica of an 18th Century weaver's cottage. It is one of several displays which show early handwork tools.

Card Weaving. The technique — also called tablet weaving — is described and illustrated with woven pieces and cards.

Chinese Embroidery. An elaborate Chinese woven robe is shown in this display, but also — typically — an embroidered medallion is shown separately, one meant to be appliquéd to a robe. Separate sleeve-band embroideries are also shown.

Mummy Wrappings. Examples of fabrics unearthed from ancient Egyptian tombs. Here, too, the construction of the fabric is detailed through informative captions.

Beadwork. A small display of examples from different regions.

Embroidery. A somewhat larger display, with examples of work from a number of countries and periods, especially muslin embroidery from India.

Netting and Tatting. A wall display showing the tools used and representative types of work produced with them.

Knitting. Chiefly a display of hand-knitting tools, but also including several handsomely carved wooden knitting "sheaths" worn by women on the right hip. They were used to hold the knitting work while the women were engaged in other household tasks. These carved sheaths were made by men as love tokens — particularly in northern England and Wales.

Needlework. An interesting display of tools, sewing cases, pin cushions, pattern books, and a fine example of stumpwork, dated 1630.

Lace. A large panel display showing many basic types, together with lace pillows and bobbins.

Peru. A small display of Inca weavings from Peru.

Printed Textiles. A small study display, showing good examples of printed fabrics from India, England, and France.

The Ulster Folk Museum at Holywood is elegantly situated in a landscaped park eight miles outside of Belfast. It is devoted to the folkways of Ulster.

BANKFIELD MUSEUM
Cont'd

Textile Tools & Machinery. Many different exhibits spread out over various parts of the museum. Among them are the following: a Burmese spinning wheel, rug looms from Nigeria and Serbia, strip-weaving looms from Ghana (Ashanti), a Chinese sandal loom, a drop-box loom, combing and carding equipment, and textile-finishing equipment.

Among the larger pieces of equipment are: a warping mill, a warping frame, late 18th-Century warping equipment used at Spitalfields, Whittaker's piecing machine (1827), and yarn-testing equipment. There are also model rooms demonstrating a cropping shop, a handweaving cottage, a spinning jenny and mule, a batten, and spinning shuttles of many different types. There is even a display of hand-cut buttons.

Tillot Blocks. These were the hand-carved wooden stamps used by textile manufacturers to mark and identify their shipping bales. The stamps are shown together with prints, and they make interesting textile-print designs in themselves.

Publications. Under the museum imprint are seven interesting monographs on textiles and textile history. A list follows.

"Costumes of Upper Burma and the Shan States" by R. A. Innes,1957 (paperback, 9½ × 7¼, 70 pages, five photographs, one in color, and 38 line drawings). Describes the Bankfield collection piece by piece, together with textile techniques used in Burma.

"The Durham Collection" by Laura E. Start, 1939 (paperback, 7¼ × 10½, 76 pages, 27 composite line drawings showing embroidery patterns in careful detail). A description of garments and embroideries from Albania and Yugoslavia in the Bankfield Museum.

"West African Narrow Strip Weaving" by Venice and Alastair Lamb, 1973. A 20-page booklet describing the collection of some 700 items assembled by the Lambs in West Africa, with four excellent photos of representative weavings from different regions.

"Non-European Looms" by R. A. Innes, 1959 (paperback, 9½ × 7¼, 74 pages). Describes 18 hand looms from Africa, 5 from India, 5 from Asia, and 1 from the Pacific (Santa Cruz). Illustrated with seven photographs of looms and over 60 line drawings of loom furniture and construction details.

"Ancient Egyptian & Greek Looms" by H. Ling Roth, 1913, reprinted 1951 (paperback, 6 × 9¼, 44 pages, 38 line drawings). This interesting early treatise by the first curator of the Bankfield Museum is, unfortunately, now out of print. It deserves to be reprinted again.

"Some Aspects of the 18th Century Woollen & Worsted Trade in Halifax" edited by Frank Atkinson, 1956 (paperback, 6 × 9, 92 pages, 6 illustrations). A fascinating document on the textile trade in the 18th Century, told through original letters and day books of Halifax merchants.

Detail of a white muslin handkerchief from Newry, County Down, c. 1840. *Ulster Folk Museum* — L685|5 (452–1973).

"Crossley Mosaics" by R. A. Innes, 1974. A small, 20-page booklet on this 19th-Century textile phenomenon, with a description of the technique, three line drawings of the equipment used, and photographs of seven representative mosaic pictures.

Postcards. The museum has also published 17 B/W postcards of pieces in its textile collection. The majority show spinning wheels and weaving equipment.

NOTE. The Bankfield collection is one unit in a series of local museums operated by the Metropolitan Borough of Calderdale, with headquarters in Clay House, Greetland, Halifax HX4 8AN. The same telephone number (Elland 2540) reaches all units. Of these, another museum of interest to textile designers and students is the newly established Piece Hall — the restoration of an early trading hall where local mills sold their "piece" goods. Not yet completed during my visit in 1974, the new Piece Hall is planned as an industrial museum with emphasis on textile manufacturing up to the introduction of steam.

HOLYWOOD

Ulster Folk Museum*
Cultra Manor, Co. Down BT18 OEU
TEL: Holywood 3555

Laura Jones, Asst. Keeper

(*"Ulster Folk & Transport Museum" is the official name, but the Transport Museum is a separate facility located in Belfast.)

The Ulster Folk Museum (not to be confused with the Ulster Museum in Belfast) is situated on an estate of 136 acres eight miles outside of Belfast. Through both indoor and outdoor exhibits it documents the traditional folkways of Ulster.

Its textile and costume collection, however, is not restricted to pieces produced in Ulster but also includes fabrics made in the

The Weaver's Cottage at Kilbarchan was formerly a weaver's home and workshop. It is now a museum of the local weaving industry (National Trust for Scotland).

Republic of Ireland. Its policy is to collect only pieces that were either made in Ireland or have some strong link with the country.

It is a large collection of some 13,500 pieces, though that figure includes a good many garments, costume accessories, and needlework tools. Most of them date from the 19th Century. Irish laces, embroidery, and linen damasks are the three strongest groups in the collection.

The lace group includes appliqué work from Carrickmacross, run-and-tambour work from Limerick, crochet lace, and needlepoint. There are many examples of lace decorations for both costume and domestic linens, as well as scarves and veils.

The embroidery group contains drawn-thread and Ayrshire work, domestic linens embroidered in Mountmellick, Berlin woolwork, an important collection of samplers (1716–1900), and the Lilley collection of embroidered handkerchiefs.

It also has an excellent group of patchwork quilts, showing traditional Irish patterns.

The linen-damask group includes both hand-and machine-woven tablecloths and napkins, as well as examples of damask cloth in all states of production.

Publications. ''The Irish Flowerers'' by Elizabeth Boyle, 1970, was published jointly by the Ulster Folk Museum and the Institute of Irish Studies. It is a comprehensive history of Irish lace and embroidery.

''Ulster Folklife'' is a museum journal, which has published a number of articles on quilting, embroidery, and lace.

''Yearbook.'' This annual museum publication has published several articles on textiles: ''Linen Industry'' (1966–7), ''Patchwork & Appliqué'' (1966–7), ''The Museum's Collection of Needlework'' (1967–8), ''Damask Weaving'' (1968–9), ''Lace'' (1969–70), and ''Needlework Tools'' (1970–71).

KILBARCHAN

The Weaver's Cottage
PA10 2AT
Mrs. A. Halifax Crawford

The Weaver's Cottage at Kilbarchan will appeal chiefly to handweavers. The town is near Paisley and was a well-known center of handweaving during the 18th and 19th Centuries. Unlike Paisley, however, it did not concentrate on jacquard weaving, and its production of fabrics remained largely a cottage industry.

Kilbarchan weavers made cambrics, muslins, lawns, silks, and shawls, but their specialty was always tartans, which lent themselves to hand-loom operation. In the 1830s there were 800 working hand looms in the town, but in the 1880s they began to give way to the power loom, and by 1900 only 200 looms were in operation. By 1950 the number had dropped to four.

The Weaver's Cottage is a substantial stone structure, built in 1723. It was the home and workshop of a Kilbarchan weaver until

Print design by the Kilkenny Workshops for Seafield Fabrics Ltd., Cork.

1940, and it reflects the history and weaving traditions of the town. The National Trust for Scotland took it over in 1954 and opened it in 1957 as a memorial museum to the local weaving industry.

Among the exhibits are weaving tools and Kilbarchan fabrics. There are shirting patterns, many tartans, and a number of locally made shawls, some of them used as bed covers. The old weaving room has been completely restored, and a local weaver demonstrates its operation on Tuesdays, Thursdays, and Saturdays from 2 to 5 P.M. He weaves skirt lengths, scarves, and head squares, mostly in tartan patterns. A reserve collection of local fabrics can be seen on request.

KILKENNY

Kilkenny Design Workshops
TEL: 056–22118

Mortimer O'Shea, Manager, Textiles

The Kilkenny Design Workshops do not hold a collection of historic textiles, but there is good reason to review their facilities. They maintain design archives of their own work and are a source of design for both professionals and students. They also design and produce prototype textiles for mills and converters.

Kilkenny is a design laboratory, established by the Government of Ireland with the aim of developing new product designs to be made and marketed by Irish manufacturers on a royalty basis (3 percent). It has been in operation for seven years (as of 1974) and has a staff of 16 resident designers, supported by an equal number of technicians and craftworkers, as well as 17 apprentices. The Workshops also draw on the talents of a panel consisting of 12 contributing designers from Ireland and other countries.

The design of fabrics for the home and contract installation — all in prototype

The Kilkenny Design Workshops are housed in late 18th Century stone buildings which were once the stables, carriage houses, and stores of the Ormonde Castle.

Kilkenny design workshops cont'd

form — is a key function of the staff, though it is also involved in the design of domestic hardware and hand tools, ceramics and glass, furniture and plastics, jewelry, silver, and packaging. The quality of work produced here has been set to a high standard, and this is maintained through an advisory panel of internationally recognized critics and designers, who pass judgment on all work before it is presented to industry.

The Workshops themselves are housed in a handsome series of late 18th-Century stone buildings, which were once the carriage houses and stables of Ormonde Castle. The place is a near idyll in the town of Kilkenny, about 70 miles south of Dublin. Here, each resident designer has a private studio and the use of general equipment for hand-weaving and hand screen printing. The Workshops have also become a training facility for young designers. A limited number of students are admitted each year, and there is provision for four scholarship places. Apprentices undergo a four-year training course, and a number of them have received scholarships for study and training abroad.

And the welcome mat is always out. Designers, manufacturers, and buyers are among the many visitors who have come from all parts of the world at an average of 250 a day during the past year. At first this invasion of visitors caused a serious disruption of work, but the management now copes with the problem through a series of demonstration units which illustrate basic hand-production methods used at the Workshops to make prototypes for commercial machine production. There is also a permanent exhibit of textiles designed at the Workshops.

During 1974, the Workshops also launched a designer-exchange program and began renovation of the nearby Kilkenny Castle Dower House as a residence hall for the program. The building will also be used as a design conference center.

LIVERPOOL

Merseyside County Museums
William Brown St. L3 8EN
TEL: (051) 207-0001

Dr. Dorothy Downes, Keeper, Antiquities; **Margaret Warhurst,** Asst. **Mrs. A. James,** Texile/Costume Dept.

At the Merseyside County Museums I was given the rare privilege of examining one of the most ancient and best preserved textiles to be seen anywhere in the world today. It is the famous girdle of Ramses III, who reigned in Egypt from 1198 to 1166 B.C.

Though the girdle is over 3,000 years old, most of it is so well preserved and it is so handsome a piece of weaving that it would be a pleasure to own and wear one like it today. It is 17 feet long, tapering gradually from a width of 5 inches down to 1⅞ inches

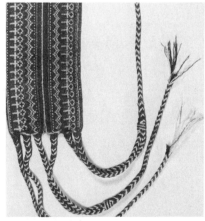

Narrow end of the Ramses III girdle. *Merseyside County Museums, Liverpool.*

at its braided tips. It is woven of fine linen yarns and is neatly patterned in soft shades of gray/green and rust. The colors are clear and subtle, though muted by time. Was it card-woven or double-woven on a loom? This issue is still ingeniously debated but unresolved by the experts.

Sadly, there is a deteriorated section several inches long at the wide end of the girdle. Orginally, this area contained an inscription written in ink, possibly by ancient Egyptians, identifying the girdle with Ramses III. A modern and overzealous attempt to intensify the writing resulted in the damage, though this may also have been abetted by the development of mold during years of storage in a steel vault. Deterioration has now been arrested by modern methods of preservation.

The Ramses girdle came to the Liverpool museum in 1867 through the bequest of Joseph Mayer, a wealthy Liverpool goldsmith with a passion for collecting antiquities. The same bequest also endowed the museum with an important collection of Coptic tapestry fragments. There are about 375 pieces in the group, many of them well preserved, and they reveal a range of Coptic weaving skill spanning the years 100 to 900 A.D. They are in the Department of Antiquities.

Among other textiles held by this department are two Tibetan temple hangings (tankas) made with appliquéd Chinese silks, several Chinese and Tibetan robes, and a small group of printed cottons from Nepal.

A different and larger group of fabrics is held by the Costume Department at the museum. It includes the following.

Near East. Embroideries from the Mediterranean and Near East, especially the Greek Islands. There are about 350 pieces in all, and they come from the much larger pioneer collection of similar fabrics assembled by the late Professor A. J. B.

RIGHT. Coptic weave from Akhmin, 4–6th Century. The tapestry work is purple wool on natural linen. *Merseyside County Museums — N61–725 (56.21.950).*

FAR RIGHT. Another Coptic tapestry fragment from Akhmin, 4–6th Century. *Merseyside — N61–756 (56.21.952).*

Wace and shared with the Victoria & Albert Museum and the Fitzwilliam Museum in Cambridge.

China. About 250 pieces, chiefly embroideries in the form of robes, sleeve bands, and mandarin squares.

England. Again, chiefly embroideries. There are several hundred pieces, including samplers, Berlin wool work, and silk embroidery of the Victorian period. Also, a number of British household fabrics, most of them with needlework.

Europe. A somewhat smaller group of European embroideries forms a good study collection.

Lace. This is the largest group in the collection and numbers at least 1,000 pieces. Except for early Venetian lace, most of the important types from European centers of lacemaking, as well as from Great Britain, are represented.

Costume. The costume collection also holds about 1,000 garments and accessories, mostly from the 19th Century. The largest number (over 500 pieces) are women's garments, but there are also about 100 children's garments and some 50 men's outfits.

From the above listings it becomes clear that Liverpool holds one of the more important but unexplored textile collections in the U. K. Students from local art schools make effective use of the collection, but it is largely unknown in the rest of the country. This is mainly due to the fact that the museum building was seriously damaged by fire bombs during World War II and has not yet been adequately restored.

As a result there is little or no exhibit space for textiles, few people have seen the collection, and a new generation of designers is largely unaware of its existence. Yet it is an important collection, administered by a cooperative staff, and well worth a trip to Liverpool.

Research Facilities

Because of space problems during the museum rebuilding program, research facilities at the museum are minimal at this time (late 1974). However, there is a fine research facility in the building immediately adjoining the museum. This is the Liverpool Central Library. It holds close to a million volumes and its high-domed, circular reference library is reminiscent of the reading room at the British Museum.

It has a good general catalog system and separate departmental libraries devoted to different areas of knowledge. The Department of Arts & Recreation is of special interest to designers and students. It has a small but excellent collection of reference books on textile design, including a number of hard-to-find early publications dealing with textiles as art. The library's technical division also has an extensive collection of books on textile technology.

Publications. "Coptic Weaves" by Margaret Seagroatt, 1965 (6¼ × 6¼ 160 pages, with 25 B/W photos of Coptic tapestry fragments and 23 diagrams illustrating Coptic weaving techniques). This is perhaps the best simple treatment I have seen on the subject. It was written by a weaver, who explains the different constructions in simple terms and with graphic diagrams. She also discusses the construction of Coptic garments, as well as dyes, yarns, and motifs.

"Liverpool Bulletin, Vol. 9," 1960–1. This issue contains an extensive article by Otfried Staudigel on "Tablet Weaving in Ancient Egypt." It presents an extensive argument (with diagrams) for Mr. Staudigel's belief that the Ramses girdle was made by tablet (card) weaving.

"Liverpool Bulletin, Vol. 10," 1961–2. This issue contains an answer to Mr. Staudigel's argument by Elisabeth Crowfoot, who believes the girdle was loom-woven. Her article is titled "Braid-Weaving Techniques

in Ancient Egypt."

The same issue of the Bulletin contains an article by Margaret Seagroatt on the museum's Coptic collection. It is a condensed version of her book, noted above.

LONDON

Bethnal Green Museum
Cambridge Heath Rd. E2 9PA
TEL: (01) 980-2415

Elizabeth Aslin, Keeper
Phyllis Fortune, Textiles/Costume

The Bethnal Green Museum is a branch of the Victoria & Albert Museum, and most of its holdings duplicate pieces which can be seen at the V & A in greater depth. But at least two good reasons justify a visit to Bethnal Green.

1. The museum building is now the most important surviving example in London of the large, light-filled, iron-and-glass prefabricated structures which were built in the 1850s and which were best typified by the Crystal Palace.

2. It focuses attention on Spitalfields silks. During most of the 18th Century and into the 19th, these fabrics — the pride of Britain's weaving tradition — were manufactured in the hamlet of Spitalfields, then close to the present location of the Bethnal Green Museum. And many of the Huguenot weavers, who worked for the Spitalfields industry, lived in crowded homes at Bethnal Green, then outside the old walls of London.

Exhibits. In the big hall of the museum about 15 original designs for Spitalfields silks are displayed, as well as some 30 examples of the fabrics themselves. Early photographs show Spitalfields looms and weavers at work. Among the displays are brief printed essays on the history of the industry.

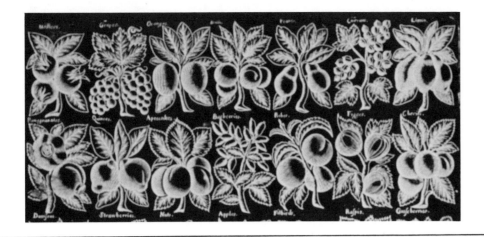

A page from the 17th Century English pattern book by Peter Stent, held by the British Museum. This photograph was made from a slide in the Fitzwilliam Museum, Cambridge.

Bethnal Green
Museum Cont'd

They told me, for example, that in the mid-18th Century Spitalfields silks (21 inches wide) sold at the high price of 10 shillings a yard for flowered patterns and up to 21 shillings for velvets or work with gold thread. I learned, too, that journeyman weavers—living in "crowded misery" at Bethnal Green—earned as little as 12 shillings a week in 1760, a year during which £233,000 worth of fabrics were exported to the American colonies alone.

In addition to the Spitalfields exhibits, Bethnal Green also displays a number of copperplate-printed cottons from the local calico printworks of Robert Jones at Old Ford, and Bromley Hall.

Costume. Aside from these displays and modest reserve stores of similar fabrics, Bethnal Green is perhaps best known for its costume collection. Some 200 outfits are on exhibit, dating from 1730 to 1960. Among them are special displays of wedding dresses, children's clothes, sportswear, and doll clothes. The dolls are representative of the superlative collection owned by the V & A and date from 1700 to modern times.

Doll Houses. It should also be mentioned that Bethnal Green has its own outstanding collection of doll houses, and these should interest designers of fabrics for the home. They provide a history of interior design in miniature.

Needlework Boxes. Equally interesting, especially to needleworkers, is a collection of superb needlework boxes dating from the 16th Century to Victorian times and showing examples of English needlework alongside the tools that made them.

The museum has a small library on the decorative arts, which is open to researchers on application. The same is true of the reserve fabrics. The curatorial staff is cooperative and knowledgeable.

LONDON

The British Museum
Great Russell St. WC1B 3DG
TEL: (01) 636-1555

The main buildings of the British Museum on Great Russell Street hold very few textiles of interest to fabric designers, but a major collection of textiles and costume is held by the British Museum's Ethnography Department, which now occupies a building of its own near Picadilly Circus. It has been renamed the Museum of Mankind and is reviewed separately under that heading.

In the Great Russell Street building a small number of historic textiles are held by each of five departments. These are briefly described below.

Egyptian Antiquities. This department holds some patterned textiles from the burial grounds of Egypt, dating from the 4th to the 12th Century A.D. and a quantity of unpatterned linen from Egypt's Dynastic Period. The more important of these pieces are displayed in the Coptic Room (1922). They include a large tapestry from Akhmin (4th–5th Century A.D.) and a square tapestry panel (5th–6th Century A.D.) with remarkably well-preserved colors.

Medieval and Later Antiquities. This department also holds a small group of Coptic textile fragments, several examples of Opus Anglicanum, a few ecclesiastical vestments, and a group of Byzantine silk fragments from the 12 and 13th Centuries.

Oriental Antiquities. A number of excavated textiles from Central Asia (the Stein Collection) and others from Egypt's Islamic Period.

Greek and Roman Antiquities. One piece of embroidered Egyptian cloth of the Late Roman Period, three fragments of asbestos cloth, and six undated fragments.

Prehistoric and Romano-British Antiquities. A few fragments of cloth attributed to the prehistoric Swiss Lake Dwellers. Also, two English fabrics from excavations in Yorkshire — one late Roman, the other Bronze Age.

The Fan Collection. The British Museum holds a renowned fan collection of the 18th and 19th Centuries, which should be of considerable interest to textile designers. It is known as the Schreiber Collection and is held in the Department of Prints & Drawings. There are over 600 pieces in the collection — a treasury of design themes from England, France, Italy, Spain, Germany, Holland, North America, and the Far East.

LONDON

Gunnersbury Park Museum
Gunnersbury Park W3 8LQ
TEL: (01) 992-2247

Bridget Goshawk, Curator

The Gunnersbury Park Museum is in West London and is easily reached by taking the Underground to the Acton Town Station. Its attraction lies in the fact that the handsome grounds and the early 19th Century mansion which houses the collections were once the home of the British Rothschild family. It also has a small but specialized collection of costumes and needlework, which are of local origin.
In all, the museum holds about 500 pieces of costume and accessories, as well as some 100 pieces of embroidery, samplers, and quilts. These were collected to illustrate life in the local region (Middlesex), and most of them date from the mid–19th to the mid–20th Century, though a few are earlier.

The collection should have special interest for designers of children's fabrics and clothing, since these form the largest group held by the museum.

The collection is accessible by appointment only, but researchers are welcomed, and all pieces have been carefully cataloged.

LONDON

Horniman Museum & Library
Forest Hill   SE23 3PQ
Tel: (01) 699-2339

Marion G. Wood, Asst. Curator

The Horniman Museum is three museums in one. Its largest section is devoted to ethnography. A second section holds one of the world's most extensive collections of musical instruments from many different cultures and periods. The third section exhibits natural-history collections of stuffed animals from every continent, as well as a good small aquarium.

This multifaceted museum stems from the private collections of a wealthy tea merchant, Frederick J. Horniman, who founded the present building in 1901 and presented it to the London County Council, which operates it through the Inner London Education Authority.

Thus, above all, the Horniman is an educational facility serving the community and attracting many groups of school children through a series of changing exhibits on special subjects.

Changing Exhibits. For example, during my visit the ethnography section was filled with excited school children examining (and drawing) a superb display of masks from more than forty regions of the world. Moreover, they were learning a great deal about the rituals and customs of other societies from informative display captions and an excellent essay on masks, which was set in large display type at the entrance to the exhibit. Textile designers would have found the exhibit equally stimulating.

Library. Still a fourth section of the Horniman is its library, which offers excellent research facilities to advanced students. It has a reference library of some 40,000 volumes, plus a photographic file of many objects in the museum collections — though only a small number on textiles.

Ethnography. The textile collection at the Horniman is held by the ethnography department and is not large as such collections go, but it is very varied and many of its holdings are choice.

Altogether, the collection consists of some 1,750 pieces and includes costume as well as flat textiles. It covers most parts of Africa, Asia, and Europe, as well as smaller areas of the Americas and Oceania. Over 75 countries and regions are represented, and the material ranges from Samoan bark cloths to Chinese court robes.

Among the larger holdings the following are represented: China — 161 pieces; Rumania — 141; India — 128; Nigeria — 105; Czechoslovakia — 96; Yugoslavia — 96; Burma — 65; Iran — 62; Ethiopia — 54; Iraq — 52; Fiji — 46; Japan — 45; Greece —45; U.S.S.R. — 41; France — 33; Jordan —33; Zaire — 30; Germany — 27; Palestine — 26; Samoa — 26; Sierra Leone —25; Turkey — 24. These are only a few of the 75 regions represented in the total collection.

Unfortunately, lack of storage space (as with London's Museum of Mankind) has made it impossible to store these textiles in the main museum building. They are kept at a warehouse in Greenwich and can therefore be examined only by special appointment.

A Kwakiutl cedar-bark cape from the northwest Pacific coast of Canada (Vancouver). It is made by twined weaving from twisted cedar-bark yarns. *Horniman Museum* — 2070.

FAR LEFT. A Pearly King suit made in the late 19th or early 20th Century. *Museum of London. — 63.7.*

LEFT. A Pantaloons costume of the early 19th Century. *Museum of London — 42.15.*

The collection in the main building is quite small and has been selected chiefly for study purposes. It consists largely of tie-dye and resist-print fabrics from North Nigeria and West Africa.

A few textiles from other regions were on exhibit in the galleries during my visit. They included embroidery from Poland; hangings from Tibet, Bali, China, and Japan; Navajo blankets; bark cloth from Tahiti; ikats from Indonesia; a Maori cloak of flax with intricate woven borders; and a rare one-piece knitted coverall from Zambia.

Note. The quickest way to reach the Horniman is by train from Charing Cross to Forest Hill Station. The bus route can be quite complicated.

LONDON

The Museum of London
Condor House,
St. Paul's Churchyard EC4M 8BE
TEL: (01) 236-2145

Kay Staniland, Curator of Costume

This is London's newest museum, still under construction at this writing (late 1974) and not scheduled to open until 1976. It replaces the London Museum in Kensington Palace and the Guildhall Museum in the City — both closed to the public since September, 1974.

The new museum will house the holdings of the two old museums in a dramatic complex of buildings erected at the corner of Aldersgate Street and London Wall, just north of St. Paul's Cathedral. It will have 50,000 square feet of exhibition galleries and will provide much more display and storage space for the major costume collection formerly housed in Kensington Palace. It will also provide modern research facilities for students.

In terms of flat textiles the collection is small: it holds less than 100 pieces of household linens and lace. But in terms of textiles-as-costume it is probably the largest in the United Kingdom — with at least 10,000 pieces and possibly as many as 20,000. No accurate count of these holdings will be possible until the collection has been transferred from the crowded basement at Kensington Palace into its expanded quarters in the new museum.

This important collection covers costume worn in London from Roman times to the present day. It is constantly increasing, especially in examples of contemporary dress, but the chief areas of its holdings are clearly defined. They fall into the following categories.

1. Archaeological. Materials excavated in the London area. They include a number of knitted caps and stockings of the Tudor period (1485–1603). Recently, the museum acquired an important group of early fabrics unearthed from an archaeological site at Baynard's Castle. They date from the 15th to the 16th Century.

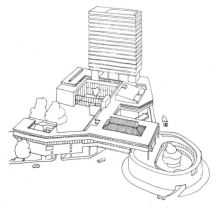

Architectural impression of the new Museum of London in St. Paul's Churchyard. It combines the former London Museum in Kensington Palace and the Guildhall Museum in the City.

2. High Fashion. This category includes fashionable clothing for both women and men, from the 16th Century to the present. It covers the output of important London couture houses, as well as those of Paris and Rome when foreign garments were worn by London people. Within the past few years the museum has also begun to collect everyday working clothes of the London population.

3. Royal. The clothing of British royalty, especially coronation garments, beginning with the reign of Charles I (1625–49). There are over 700 pieces in this group, including some 20 dresses belonging to Queen Victoria and spanning her lifetime.

4. Theatrical. This is the largest collection of theatrical costumes in the U. K. A number were designed for Sir Henry Irving, and the emphasis is on costumes from Shakepeare productions. There are some 300 garments and accessories in this group.

5. Uniforms. This group covers both military and civil uniforms, including British ceremonial robes of the Church, the Law, the Court, and the City, as well as the uniforms of London police, firemen, postmen, and a typical "Pearly King" suit.

6. Accessories. A wide range of smaller pieces which supplement all the above categories.

Unfortunately, these rich holdings will be inaccessible until the collection is housed in the new museum. Until that time, researchers must be satisfied with eight published catalogs describing different parts of the collection. They are listed below.

Publications. "Coronation Costume & Accessories 1685–1953," 1973 (69 pages, 25 photographs, 2 in color).

"Women's Costume 1600–1750," 1969 (43 pages, 21 photographs and two dress patterns).

"Women's Costume 1750–1800," 1972 (71 pages, 28 photographs).

The William Morris Gallery in the Walthamstow section of London. It was the former Morris family home where he lived from 1848–56.

"Men's Costume 1580–1750," 1970 (51 pages, 25 photographs.)

"Men's Costume 1750–1800," 1973 (58 pages, 22 photographs.)

"Stage Costume & Accessories," 1967 (94 pages, 29 photographs).

"Elizabeth R.," 1971 (16 pages, 17 photographs). A picture booklet illustrating costumes used in the TV series of that name.

"Mary Quant's London," 1973 (32 pages, 39 photographs). Catalog of an exhibition held at the museum in 1973.

LONDON

William Morris Gallery
Forest Rd., Walthamstow E17 4PP
TEL: (01) 527-5544   Ext 390

Norah C. Gillow, Asst. in Charge
Peter W. Megoran, Senior Asst.

A visit to the William Morris Gallery in Walthamstow is something of a pilgrimage for anyone interested in the man's work and the craft-revival movement with which he is identified.

Walthamstow is in the eastern section of London (Borough of Waltham Forest) and easy enough to reach by Underground. The Gallery is housed in a large brick mansion surrounded by Lloyd Park. It is not a particularly interesting building, but it was the wealthy home where Morris lived as a youth (1848–56). Walthamstow was then a rural area, and the present Lloyd Park was the grounds of the mansion which then extended for half a mile to the edge of Epping Forest. It is now a working-class district.

The Collection. The Gallery is filled with the work of Morris and his associates in the company he headed. For textile designers the chief interest will be the home-furnishings fabrics and wallpapers produced by the firm — many of them designed by Morris himself.

To a contemporary designer the fabric lengths stored in the Gallery may be disappointing at first glance. They do not have the impact or the crisp detail of the same designs reproduced in books. However, this is because the examples held by the museum are frequently old and faded with use. A much stronger impression is given by an examination of the Morris & Co. sample books, which the Gallery also owns. Here the colors are sharper and clearer. To my eye the best designs are the single-color prints, which have a sophistication and a flow of design that seems quite contemporary.

It is also interesting to discover that the prices at which these fabrics were sold in the 1890s ranged from about 6 shillings for a 36-inch heavy cotton to about 11 shillings for a 54-inch linen. They were therefore relatively expensive by the standards of their time.

In all, the museum holds over 400 designs created either by Morris or his associates — most of them in the last quarter of the 19th Century. They include 122 printed textiles, 62 woven textiles, 89 wallpapers, and 80 original designs on paper. There are also two chintz pattern books and seven wallpaper sample books. The museum also holds 85 textiles designed by A.H. Mackmurdo, an architect and designer who was associated with Morris and who continued to work in the same tradition after Morris died in 1896.

Research Facilities. The museum has published complete catalogs of its holdings and has a fair representation of its pieces in photographs. It also has a study room and a library of about 1,000 volumes on applied arts of the period.

For those who are interested, a collection of books designed by Morris and printed at his famous Kelmscott Press are held in the museum safe.

Publications. "Catalogue of the Morris Collection," 1969 (76 pages, five photographs). A complete description of all items in the collection, together with biographical and historical notes and bibliography.

"Catalogue of the A.H. Mackmurdo and Century Guild Collection," 1967 (35 pages, six photographs). The Century Guild was an association of craftsmen and a vehicle for the craft-revival movement.

Evenlode chintz, a print designed by William Morris in 1883. The William Morris Gallery holds many such prints. *V & A — L 2322 (Circ. 93–1933).*

A fine example of beadwork from South Africa, probably made in the late 19th Century. *Museum of Mankind — XVI–20.*

LONDON

Museum of Mankind
(Dept. of Ethnography, Br. Museum)
6 Burlington Gardens WIX 2EX
TEL: (01) 437-2224

Bryan Cranstone, Deputy Keeper

The Museum of Mankind may well hold one of largest and most important collections of textiles and costume in the United Kingdom. I say "may" because it is impossible to determine even its approximate size. No count has ever been made of the accessions (which are constantly growing), and the closest I can come to an estimate is to say that it may be in the range of 10,000 pieces.

In exploring the accession records at the museum I was fascinated to discover the method by which entries are made. There is no card-index system. All accessions are entered in large, black ledgers which resemble old account books. They are entered by hand with pen and ink. Each object is carefully described, and each description is accompanied by a meticulous pen-and-ink drawing of the object described. The drawings are exact, and many are quite beautiful. To discover such an anachronism in this era of electronic technology is refreshing — though it leaves something to be desired as far as research is concerned.

Another obstacle to exploration of the textile collection is the storage problem. Most of its pieces are not currently in the Burlington Gardens museum but are stored in a warehouse at Shoreditch. This reserve store can be examined on application, and there are plans for a study room in the Shoreditch facility, but present arrangements do not encourage research. This will probably change for the better within the next few years as the museum reorganizes its facilities and its holdings.

In the meantime a researcher must largely depend on the museum's changing exhibits, which are excellent and have resulted in the valuable research-oriented publications noted later. There is also a small reserve store of textiles and costume in the Burlington Gardens building, and this can be seen on application.

Ethnographic Collections.

As to the collections themselves, they fall into an area usually referred to as ethnographic — often misnamed "primitive." In the main this means they were collected by anthropologists rather than by textile specialists, are generally late 19th Century or comtemporary in date, and come from societies which have not yet achieved the dubious benefits of industrialization. As to being "primitive," I reject the use of the word entirely, since I consider many of these textiles to be among the most sophisticated and visually exciting artifacts produced by any culture, ancient or modern. (Think of double ikats from Indonesia or Kente cloths from Ghana.)

The textile/costume collection at the Museum of Mankind falls into four categories, each under the care of a separate curator. Highlights from the four groups are listed below, together with the names of the curators currently in charge of each area.

Europe/Asia (Shelagh Weir, Asst. Keeper). The textiles in this category were described to me as numbering in the thousands. The largest group consists of batik, ikat, and tie-dye fabrics from Indonesia and India. There are also brocades from Malay and ikats from Sumba. Other sources are Sarawak, Thailand, Assam (Naga Tribe), and Bokhara.

From Persia (Iran) come woven and embroidered cloths made by village craftworkers, a number from the Turkoman region. West Pakistan is represented by rugs from Baluchistan. There are woven and embroidered fabrics from Greece, Turkey, and Cyprus. A particularly important collection consists of Arab peasant embroidery and weaving from Palestine (before 1948).

There is embroidery work from Bulgaria and China and several examples of Ainu appliqué work from North Japan.

In short, a wide-ranging and very stimulating collection.

The Americas (Elizabeth Carmichael, Asst. Keeper). This may be the largest category in the textile collection, since it is estimated at over 5,000 pieces. It does not cover all ethnographic areas of the Americas but has good representation from a number of regions.

For example, the Peruvian collection is considered the most extensive in the U. K. and is especially strong in fabrics from Paracas and Tiahuanaco. From North America there are textiles made by Indian tribes in the Northwest, the Plains, and the Woodlands. There are good examples of quillwork embroidery and Navajo rugs, a particularly fine group of molas from the San Blas Indians of Panama, and a still larger group of contemporary weavings from Guatemala.

Most of these pieces and many other smaller holdings are currently stored in the museum warehouse at Shoreditch.

Pacific/Oceania (Bryan Cranstone, Deputy Keeper). Over 1,000 pieces make up this collection of fabrics from many areas in the Pacific. Among the regions represented are Melanesia, New Zealand, Polynesia, New Guinea, New Ireland, New Hebrides, the Solomons, New Caledonia, and Hawaii.

The largest and most important group in this category consists of tapa cloths from many of the areas listed above. The designs are varied and should have strong appeal to print designers.

Equally important is a collection of feather cloaks from Hawaii. These are the cere-

Another example of beadwork design, this one from India, probably late 19th Century. *Museum of Mankind — LI–5.*

monial garments of tribal chieftains, large in scale and brilliant in color, with big abstract motifs of circles, lozenges, and crescents. Their designs are often reminiscent of those in Halloween pumpkins.

Another interesting group of fabrics comes from the Maori tribes of New Zealand. Many of these are finger-woven of flax yarns to form bands and kilts.

Africa (John Picton, Assistant Keeper). There are about 800 pieces in this collection, and they come from many regions on the African continent. The largest groups are from Nigeria and Sierra Leone, but there are representative pieces from Ghana, Senegal, Mali, Morocco, Algeria, Ethiopia, Uganda, Kenya, Abyssinia, Liberia, and Zaire. Most of them are in the form of garments with elaborate woven, printed, and embroidered designs.

An interesting self-contained group within the African collection came to the museum in the bequest of C. A. Beving, a Manchester textile merchant. Manchester has long been an important resource for printed cotton textiles exported to Africa, and Mr. Beving traveled widely in Africa and collected native textiles, which he used as a source of print design. There are 432 pieces of textiles and costume in the Beving bequest, and they include both the original source material and lengths of the printed textiles derived from them.

Library. If firsthand research facilities are currently inadequate at the Museum of Mankind, this is partially offset by a fine library of ethnographic works dealing with all regions and societies represented in the collections. Some 15,000 books and pamphlets are available to researchers, including a complete file of the Ciba Review, which is a notable resource on textile design, history, and technology.

Publications. "Palestinian Embroidery" by Shelagh Weir, 1970 (44 pages, 8¼" x 8¼", 31 photographs, 6 in color). A schol-

arly and informative discussion of traditional embroidery work made by the Arab fellahin women of Palestine. The material shown here was the theme of an important exhibit at the museum.

"Spinning & Weaving in Palestine" by Shelagh Weir, 1970 (40 pages, 8¼" x 8¼", 25 photographs, 6 in color). Explains the textile craftwork of Palestinian Arabs as practiced from the second half of the 19th Century until 1948. It covers fibers, spinning, dyeing, and the different types of equipment used.

Cotton stencil print, Nigeria (Yoruba). *Museum of Mankind — 1953AF (17.18).*

"Village Arts of Romania" 1971 (48 pages, 8¼" x 8¼", 30 photographs, 10 in color). This is the catalog of a loan exhibition from the Romanian government held at the museum in 1971. It covers all village crafts, but features textiles and costume.

Photographs. The museum publishes an excellent series of color postcards on Palestinian Arab embroidery. Also available are about 30 color transparencies (35 mm) of textiles — chiefly from Africa, Indonesia, and Peru.

Hawaiian feather cloak, mid-19th Century. *Museum of Mankind — V–19.*

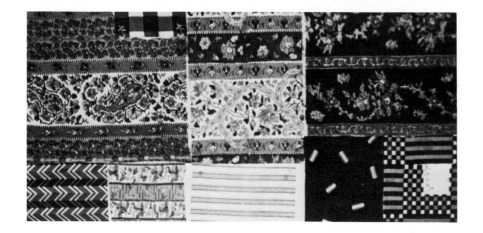

A page of print swatches from a 19th Century mill sample book in the research library at the Textile School of the Royal College of Art, London.

LONDON

RCA Textile School
Kensington Gore SW7 2EU
TEL: (01) 584-5020

Prof. Roger Nicholson, Director

The Textile School at the Royal College of Art is a graduate school, widely recognized as the leading institution in the U. K. for training textile designers. Its facilities are not open to the public, but its director, Professor Roger Nicholson, has assured me that its research library will be made accessible to qualified researchers if they apply in advance.

Sample Books. This research library holds a small treasure trove of historic fabrics in the form of bound sample books. In all, there are 36 bound volumes of swatches dating from 1820 to 1909. Most of them were formerly in the possession of Britain's Textile Council, successor to the Cotton Board, which was based in Manchester. The Textile Council bequeathed them to the Royal College of Art.

These volumes form a record of textiles produced in Great Britain during most of the 19th Century. They include small swatches of woven fabrics, often no more than 2 inches square, and larger samples of printed cloth, sometimes 12 inches square. Most of the volumes are about 14 by 21 inches in size and from 4 to 9 inches thick. They contain many thousands of samples.

Some of the books show fabrics from specific firms — notably Geo. P. & J. Baker of London and the Swaisland Printworks of Crawford, Kent. But most of them represent anonymous producers, whose fabrics of record were collected through the years by the Cotton Board and held as a national archive. Nor are the fabrics only cotton: British wools and silks are also preserved, as well as a substantial number of textiles made in France.

Burne-Jones Collection. I found these large volumes most interesting as a source of textile-design ideas, but even more interesting to my eye were three smaller books also held by the research library. They come from the private library of Edward Burne-Jones, the painter, tapestry designer, and associate of William Morris. These three books are Japanese, accordion-folded in the Japanese manner, and bound in figured silk. And they contain some 400 superb examples of Japanese silk weaving, which are as fine as anything I have yet seen in museum collections.

The examples are not dated, but I would place them in the late 18th and early 19th Centuries. I like to think Burne-Jones himself selected and mounted them in these handsome portfolios, possibly as a source of future design ideas for his paintings and tapestries, but perhaps simply because he saw them as beautiful examples of textile design and consummate weaving skill. For me, they represent one of the richest sources of textile design it has yet been my pleasure to examine.

Page from one of the portfolios in the Burne-Jones collection described above.

LONDON

Victoria & Albert Museum
South Kensington SW7 2RL
TEL: (01) 589-6371

Donald King, Keeper, Textile Dept.
Natalie Rothstein, Deputy Keeper

I am reluctant to describe any institution as the "biggest," the "first," or the "leading" one of its kind. Such value judgments can usually be challenged. Yet, in discussing the textile collection at the Victoria & Albert Museum, I find it difficult to avoid terms of this order.

After spending the better part of three working weeks exploring its facilities and comparing them with those of other major collections, I became convinced that the V & A now holds the richest and the most accessible collection of historic textiles in the world.

The measure of its importance becomes apparent in the following statistics.

1. It is one of the world's largest collection of historic textiles—not counting small and generally more contemporary sample swatches, which a few other museums own in vast numbers. For example, the Musée de l'Impression Sur Etoffes in Mulhouse, France has some 6 million such swatches, and the Brooklyn Museum in New York owns perhaps 3 million. The V & A holds about 40,000 pieces, of which less than 4,000 are costume, plus some 10,000 textile designs on paper.

2. In range it covers almost 5,000 years — from the 3rd millennium B.C. to the present — and it documents most known techniques used to construct or decorate a fabric.

3. Its scope is vast. It owns pieces from almost every important textile-producing culture and period whose artifacts survive.

RIGHT. Springtime view of the main entrance to the Victoria & Albert Museum from Cromwell Road, London.

FAR RIGHT. Entrance to the Textile Study Rooms in the northeast corner of the Victoria & Albert Museum.

I say "almost," because the V & A consciously avoids collecting "primitive" textiles of the type usually held by museums of anthropology.

4. The depth and quality of its acquisitions are world-renowned. It holds not a few, but usually many examples — and those choice — of all fabric types from most periods of history. It is therefore an exceptionally rich and rewarding collection for the designer.

5. Equally if not more important to designers is the accessibility of the collection. It is well organized and definitively cataloged. Facilities for the study of historic textile design are unsurpassed at the V & A, as will become evident.

6. Thirteen spacious galleries in the museum are devoted exclusively to permanent displays of woven fabrics, printed fabrics, lace, embroidery, tapestry, and carpets.

7. These 13 galleries expose more than 3,000 textiles on walls, screens, and in pull-out frames. The frames are stored in file cabinets, from which they can easily be removed for detailed study or for photographing. Many of the larger pieces are covered with movable curtains to protect them against fading. All textiles on display carry informative captions. In effect, the V & A is a self-service facility for the study of textiles.

8. There are subsidiary displays of textiles and/or costume in over fifty other galleries throughout the museum. Here they find a logical place among the decorative arts of a particular period or country.

9. The importance assigned to textiles at the V & A is indicated by the fact that the Department of Textiles has a curatorial staff of twelve people. Add to this other textile specialists in the Indian Section, the Far Eastern Section, and the Circulation Department, which is responsible for traveling exhibitions.

10. The Textile Department has four storage rooms to house different parts of the reserve collections. One of them (Room 110) is a huge, skylit gallery containing some 2,000 large file drawers of carefully indexed textiles. Normally, all material is accessible by appointment, though larger pieces may be seen only when staff is available to handle them.

11. The Students' Room of the Indian Section (off Room 28) also holds a reserve store of at least 3,000 textiles, and these, too, are easily available to researchers by appointment.

12. The Department of Prints & Drawings holds a major portion of the 10,000 textile designs on paper which the museum owns.

13. The Costume Collection (administered by the Department of Textiles) holds about 1,500 full ensembles and 2,000 fashion accessories. It has a large permanent display in the circular Costume Court.

14. The Photograph Sales Section has on file the photographs of record for approximately 9,000 V & A textiles, together with about 200 color transparencies. These are filed by type, country, and period.

15. The National Art Library (a part of the V & A) is considered the world's largest art reference library — with half a million books, pamphlets, and periodicals, as well as a photograph reference file of some 200,000 pictures.

* * *

This statistical listing is no more than a bare-boned index of the vast resources available to textile designers and students at the V & A. A more detailed description of the collection follows.

Highlights of the V & A Textile Collection

Over the main entrance to the V & A, carved in stone, is the following inscription:

"The Excellence of Every Art Must Consist in the Complete Accomplishment of its Purpose."

It was to improve this "purpose" that the Government School of Design (predecessor to the V & A) was founded in 1837. Its conscious aim was to elevate the design standards of British industrial art. To this end, examples of "good" textile design were acquired as early as 1842. Among the first acquisitions were European fabrics of the Middle Ages and the 16th to the 17th Century.

In 1909, the present museum building was opened, with space to house large textile acquisitions, including the important collections of Bock (1864) and Forrer (1899). Today, all textiles and textile designs owned by the V & A are distributed between five museum departments:

1. The Department of Textiles
2. The Circulation Department
3. The Indian Section
4. The Far Eastern Section
5. The Department of Prints & Drawings

Highlights from the resources of these different departments are reviewed in the following sections.

Before 1500 A.D. — Woven & Embroidered

The earliest textiles owned by the V & A date from the 3rd to the 1st millennium B.C. These are chiefly from Egypt, and they include several dozen pieces of plain linen, as well as a few overshirts and fragments with woven patterning. There is also a rare embroidery of the 5th Century B.C. from Attica.

Egypt from the 3rd Century A.D. is superbly represented by a major group of close to 2,500 textiles. The largest number are Coptic tapestry fragments, but there are also several complete tunics with tapestry bands, a number of resist-dyed linens,

Victoria & Albert Museum Cont'd

patterned silk/wool fabrics, and embroideries. In addition to fabrics made by the Christian Copts there are also several hundred pieces made by the Muslims of ancient Egypt.

Near Eastern and Central Asiatic textiles up to the 11th Century (mostly of silk) form a smaller group, but the examples are choice.

The famous Bayeux Tapestry (11th Century) can also be seen at the V & A — all 70 meters of it. Not the actual tapestry, of course, since that is in Bayeux, France, but a photographic facsimile in full scale and full color, ingeniously housed in a glass-topped case (Room 107). The reproduction has been rolled as a scroll and connected to an electric motor. At the touch of a lever it unrolls slowly under the glass.

Textiles from the 12th to the 15th Century are represented by European ecclesiastical pieces, famous examples of Opus Anglicanum in the Clare chasuble and Syon cope, German and Italian embroidery, and several hundred examples of Italian silk weaving.

Ancient Peru is represented by about 100 pieces, mostly fragments from the pre-Conquest period.

16th Century — Woven

Some 1,500 woven fabrics in the collection date from the 16th Century. The most sumptuous of these are velvets — plain and many-colored, often voided and brocaded with gold thread. Most are from the great Italian weaving centers of this period and are chiefly ecclesiastical — copes, dalmatics, chasubles, etc.

The V & A also holds 27 decorated linen towels of the type made in Perugia during the 16th Century. Also a varied group of smaller pieces which document the rich silk damasks, brocatelles, and woolen velvets of the period.

17th Century — Woven

Over 2,000 fabrics in the collection reflect the costly tastes of the 17th Century. Again, the majority come from Italy, which dominated the production of luxurious textiles until after the middle of the century, when French silks began to compete.

This group contains both apparel and home-furnishings fabrics. The apparel fabrics include a number of ecclesiastical vestments, bearing mantles for christenings, ribbons, garters, silk purses, and other small-patterned cloths.

The home-furnishings group has brocaded silks and damasks used in royal bed chambers and some less elaborate weavings from more modest homes of the period. Some of these fabrics are blends of silk/linen, silk/wool, or linen/wool. There is also an important group of 17th-Century table linens, consisting of about 75 pieces with complicated Biblical and floral designs. They were woven in Holland, Belgium, and Germany.

During the 17th Century fashions in textile design began to change frequently, and these changes can be traced in the collection. There are many good examples of the Persian influence, the vogue for chinoiserie, and the baroque trend.

18th Century — Woven

An even larger group of about 2,500 pieces dates from the 18th Century, with special emphasis on the elaborate silk weavings of Lyon in France and Spitalfields in England. The depth of these groups makes it possible to follow style changes almost from season to season. There are velvets, damasks, silks brocaded in gold and silver, and complicated colored silk weaves of great technical ingenuity. Similarly elaborate silks can be seen in about 50 eclesiastical vestments of this period.

Textile designers emerged from anonymity during the 18th Century, and the V & A holds many fabrics whose designers are known—Jean Revel, Phillippe de Lasalle, and Anna Maria Garthwaite, among others.

The silk weavings of Spitalfields are especially well documented, since about 1,000 of the original dated paper designs have survived, many of them held in the Department of Prints & Drawings at the V & A. The Textile Department holds about 120 of these Spitalfields fabrics, and some of them can be compared with the original designs.

Other 18th-Century textiles include more than 100 table-linen damasks from Holland, Flanders, Germany, Scotland, and Ireland; a number of woolen fabrics made in Norwich for export; and a group of traditional sashes worn by the Polish aristocracy during this period.

19th Century — Woven

The collection of some 2,000 woven textiles from the 19th Century contains many pieces acquired at the European commercial exhibitions which proliferated during a period of great industrial expansion. The most important come from the Great Exhibition of 1851 held at the Crystal Palace in London. Among the strong French group are many silks from renowned Lyon weavers — dress and home-furnishings fabrics, ribbons, shawls, and pictures.

The British group is well represented by the products of commercial firms, such as Warner & Sons of Spitalfields, and by leading textile designers of the period, such as Pugin, Owen Jones (who authored "The Grammar of Ornament"), Christopher Dresser, Bruce Talbert, Lindsay Butterfield, and Walter Crane. Most of the woven textiles designed by William Morris and J. H. Dearle are in the collection — as well as printed textiles by the same designers, to be noted later.

Section of the Near East Study Room at the V & A. The walls are covered with framed examples. Others are stored in the file cabinet.

Among other important British textile producers represented are the Scottish firm of Morton & Co., A. H. Lee of Birkenhead, Silver Studios, Century Guild, and Liberty. There are many Art Nouveau textiles, including the work of C. F. A. Voysey, Lewis F. Day, Sidney Mawson, Harry Napper, and Arthur Silver.

Silk ribbons and woven silk pictures — both specialities of Coventry firms — reflect an intriguing aspect of 19th-Century taste, and the collection has at least 100 pieces of this genre. The shawl industries of both Paisley and Norwich are well represented with a large number of pieces, and it is illuminating to note the subtle differences between these skillful machine-made weavings and the hand-made Kashmir shawls they attempted to duplicate with only moderate success. The Kashmir shawls are held by the Indian Section.

20th Century — Woven, Printed, and Embroidered

The trends in textile design from 1900 to the present are revealed in a collection of about 2,500 woven, printed, and embroidered textiles.

British Art Nouveau fabrics form a large group, with representative pieces from designers such as Voysey, Walter Crane, and Ann Macbeth. There are textiles from the Omega Workshops (1913–1919), designed by Vanessa Bell and Roger Fry. Other name designers in the 20th-Century group include Henry Moore, Duncan Grant, Paul Nash, Enid Marx, and Ethel Mairet — all with home furnishings. There are American textiles from Stehli Silks and French textiles designed by Raoul Dufy, Robert Bonfils, and Sonia Delaunay. Also a group of award-winning British fabrics by Graham Sutherland, Marino Marini, and John Piper, as well as a number of Op and Pop designs. Contemporary tapestries can also be seen in the collection,

notably the work of Jean Lurçat, Alexander Calder, Archie Brennan, Gerald Laing, and Harold Cohen.

Embroidery — After 1500 A.D.

The embroidery collection held by the Department of Textiles contains some 3,000 pieces. They range in size and technique from table carpets to pin cushions and from heavy canvaswork to delicately embroidered muslins. All the countries of Western Europe are represented. (Embroideries from India and the Far East are held by the Indian and Far Eastern Sections.)

English embroidery is the strongest group in the collection, beginning with domestic embroidery of the 16th and 17th Centuries. This includes the famous Bradford and Gifford table carpets, and fragments from the Oxburgh Hangings. Later 17th-Century pieces include a large number of samplers, several embroidered caskets, and embroidered pictures.

From the 18th Century come several elaborate bed sets, embroidered with silk and metal threads, as well as heavy canvas embroideries for carpets and chair seats. Quilts and coverlets of the 18th Century are very well represented, and there is an especially important group of about 50 English patchwork quilts dating from the late 18th to the late 19th Century. Ecclesiastical vestments form another important group, with about 100 pieces from the 17th and 18th Centuries.

One of the largest embroidery groups in the collection comes from the Greek Islands, dated 17th to 19th Century. There are about 900 pieces, mainly from the pioneer collections of Professors R. M. Dawkins and Alan Wace.

Another large group is Turkish in origin, including many very fine embroidered silk costumes dating from the 16th to the 19th Century. Other countries of the Near East — principally Persia (Iran) and

Syria — are represented by several hundred pieces, some of which are exquisitely woven silks and velvets.

European peasant embroidery is somewhat fragmentary, but there are choice examples from the Mediterranean area, Yugoslavia, Hungary, the Balkans, Germany, Scandinavia, and the U.S.S.R.

Printed Fabrics

There are some 4,000 printed and dyed pieces held by the Department of Textiles, and this does not include the large group held by the Indian Section. The range is very wide — from resist-dyed Coptic fabrics to modern screen prints.

The major part of this large collection is English and French in origin and dates from the second half of the 18th Century to the latter part of the 19th Century. There are plate-printed cottons made by Robert Jones at Old Ford as early as 1761 and many French Toiles de Jouy, notably a large number of designs by the renowned Jean-Baptiste Huet of the Oberkampf printworks. Many of the French examples were acquired from the Mayoux Collection in 1919.

Also well represented are the printed fabrics of William Morris, as well as those of many other leading designers, some of whose names have already been noted in previous paragraphs on the 20th-Century collections.

Tapestries

Over 200 tapestries are held by the V & A. The most important ones date from the 15th and early 16th Centuries. Among them are the four large Devonshire Hunting Tapestries, which were probably woven at Tournai about 1440. They are shown in the museum's Gothic Tapestry Court. Other tapestries displayed here include one piece of The Trojan War tapestries (1472)

A section of Room 96 at the V & A. Half the room is devoted to a lace display which exhibits some 300 examples of the craft from many areas and times.

and three Brussels tapestries — The Triumphs of Petrarch. Additional galleries are devoted to changing exhibitions of English, French, and Flemish tapestries of the 17th to the 18th Century.

Lace

The lace collection contains over 2,500 pieces. They range from lacis (network) covers of the 16th Century to complex machine laces of the 20th Century. The collection is exceptionally rich in Italian needle lace of the 17th Century. There are also many fine examples of bobbin lace from the 18th Century, particularly from Brussels. The bulk of the collection is composed of "fashion" laces, but it does not neglect peasant laces from European countries, as well as work from South America, India, and the East Indies. There are also some exquisite examples of tatting.

Costume

The V & A costume collection (not including pieces at Bethnal Green) consists of some 1,500 full ensembles and about 2,000 costume accessories, among them many children's garments. A permanent display of selected costumes can be seen in the large, circular Costume Court, where 104 dresses and 30 suits illustrate the fashion continuum from 1700 to 1948. In reserve store are 550 dresses and 55 suits covering a period from 1720 to 1970. Highlights of the collection include the Firbank acquisition of garments by turn-of-the-century English couturiers, and the Cecil Beaton acquisition, which reflects French haute couture of the recent past and consists of about 750 dresses, suits, and accessories.

There is also a large and fascinating collection of dolls, from 1700 to the present, many of them with extensive wardrobes.

Carpets

There are approximately 1,600 carpets and carpet fragments in the V & A, dating from the 9th to the 20th Century. They represent work from Persia (Iran), Turkey, China, Chinese Turkestan, India, North Africa, and Europe. The most important pieces are probably those from Persia, Turkey, and India, dating from the 16th and 17th Centuries. Among the most famous are the Persian Ardabil Carpet made in 1539–40, the Chelsea Carpet (Persia, 16th Century), and the Fremlin Carpet (India, early 17th Century).

Swatch & Pattern Books

In addition to the impressive resources listed in the previous paragraphs, the Department of Textiles also holds a large and varied range of swatch and pattern books, which document textile-design trends in many types of fabrics and for many periods.

For example: 33 Lyon silk designs, dated 1761–1771; three books of designs for woven silks by Anna Maria Garthwaite, dated 1743–4; and 139 point papers, dated 1785–1901.

Another important holding consists of 17 production ledgers from Warner & Sons Ltd., a leading British producer of home-furnishings fabrics. They cover the period 1884–1930 and contain a sample of every fabric woven by the firm during those years.

Among other design resources are 76 pattern books of British textile firms, some dating back to the 18th Century and one showing Norwich worsteds made in 1763; 20 pattern books of Spitalfields silk manufacturers, 1773–1859; a 1764 French order book for silks; a large volume showing woven fabrics stocked by the firm of Morris & Co.; and three books of woven ribbons from the early and mid-19th Century.

These represent only a sampling of many similar design resources held by the Department of Textiles. Among them is one I find particularly intriguing, because it is a personal record of early British textile trends. (Intriguing also because it was only recently acquired by the V & A, having been graciously relinquished by the original purchaser, Colonial Williamsburg.) It is an album of fabric swatches put together by one Barbara Johnson between 1746 and 1823. It shows cuttings and prices of 122 English fabrics which she had made up into dresses for herself in the north of England, where her father was Vicar of Olney.

Far Eastern Textiles

The Far Eastern Section of the V & A holds one of the world's major collections of Chinese fabrics — about 4,000 pieces, divided almost equally between woven and embroidered textiles. Its greatest strength lies in pieces from the 17th to the 19th Century, but it also has important examples of Chinese textile art from the Han Dynasty (206 B.C.–220 A.D.) and from the Tang Dynasty (618–900 A.D.).

Medieval Chinese textiles are well represented, and there are some extraordinarily beautiful silk tapestries (k'o-ssu) from the Ming Dynasty (1368–1644).

The greatest scope and variety, however, is found in fabrics from the Ching Dynasty (1644–1912). These include some incredibly fine embroideries, k'o-ssu, velvets, brocades, and a rich collection of some 250 robes, representing the wide range of status and purpose which such gorgeous apparel denoted.

Japanese textiles are somewhat less impressively represented, but the Far Eastern Section has fine examples of Noh robes, priests' robes (kesa), gift covers (fukusas), embroideries, woven textiles, and silk tapestries. It also holds a number of resist-dyed fabrics from rural Japan — less exotic

A section of Primary Gallery 41 at the V & A. Here are displayed many fine examples of textile art from India.

than the court textiles but perhaps more important for contemporary designers. Equally interesting to designers is a group of small-patterned, 19th-Century woven silk jacquards with subtle arrangements of geometric figures.

Indian Textiles

The Indian Section of the V & A inherited the private museum of the East India Company, which was taken over in 1858 by the Secretary of State for India and was then expanded to emphasize handicrafts. It is therefore rich in examples of the traditional textile crafts and holds several thousand pieces representing every facet of India's imaginative textile culture.

The collection covers woven, printed, painted, and embroidered fabrics from the 17th to the 20th Century. They fall into three main categories: (1) court fabrics, (2) home-market fabrics, and (3) export fabrics.

Court fabrics are among the earliest in the collection and are therefore very rare and understandably few in number. Among them are some intricately embroidered hangings.

Home market fabrics include many garments, peasant embroideries, and bandhana work (tie-dye), as well as both woven and printed yardage in cotton and silk. There is also a large group of silk and gold saris from the main weaving centers of India.

Export fabrics are represented by one of the world's most extensive and comprehensive collections of chintz produced in India and sold in Europe by the East India companies during the 17th and 18th Centuries.

Equally important are the fine collections of Kashmir shawls and sheer Dacca muslins, many of them embroidered.

The Indian Section holds about 100 pieces of Javanese batik, as well as smaller groups of textiles from Afghanistan, Tibet, and Burma. Also a large number of hand-carved wooden blocks used in textile printing.

The Textile Study Rooms

Some of the finest and most representative pieces from the categories described in previous sections of this review are on display or are easily available in the halls and study rooms of the Textile Department, the Indian Section, and the Far Eastern Section.

The study rooms and exhibition halls of the Textile Department are concentrated in the northeast corner of the museum, one flight up from the entrance floor. Here, a series of ten galleries is arranged in the following order.

Hall 107. Here is the Bayeux Tapestry reproduction.

Hall 109. A long corridor displaying some of the collection's finest embroidered English coverlets of the 18th Century. Also 17th-Century embroideries.

Rooms 100, 101. The door to these two adjoining rooms opens into six connecting textile study rooms, which are open 10 A.M. to 6 P.M. Monday through Saturday and 2:30 to 6 P.M. on Sunday. However, researchers should note that the cabinets which hold framed textile panels are locked at 4:30 on weekdays, at 12:30 on Saturdays, and all day on Sundays.

Displayed on walls and standing screens or stored in frame cabinets are some 2,000 textiles on permanent exhibit in these two large galleries. They can be examined at leisure without consulting members of the curatorial staff. Fabrics in the frame cabinets can be taken to adjoining work tables for more careful study. Photography and drawing are allowed. All pieces are informatively captioned, often with historical notes on design and construction.

Room 100 is devoted entirely to woven textiles, chiefly European, and it illustrates the development of pattern design from classical times to the beginning of the 20th Century. Also displayed is a small group of pre-Columbian textiles from Peru.

Room 101 is divided into three sections: (1) English embroidery, (2) Continental European embroidery, and (3) printed textiles.

Room 99. This area is given over to textiles of the Near East. Work from Turkey and Persia (Iran) predominates, but some of the frame cabinets hold fine pieces from Syria, Bokhara, and a few other Near Eastern countries. There is an especially fine display of Near Eastern costume in brocaded and embroidered silks. Cabinets of framed panels expand the display, as in other rooms. In all, Room 99 holds about 300 examples of woven silks, velvets, embroidery, and costume. (A few other fine examples are displayed in the Primary Galleries, devoted to the art of Islam — Rooms 42 and 47B.)

Hall 102. A long corridor (like 109) displays eight unique English patchwork quilts of the late 18th and early 19th Centuries.

Room 98. The Far Eastern textile study room. It holds over 300 examples of textile art, mostly from China and Japan, dating from the 3rd to the 19th Century. Fabrics are displayed on walls and screens, as well as on frame panels. There are truly magnificent examples of embroidery, silk tapestry, Mandarin squares, sleeve bands, and other work of consummate skill. Also displayed are a number of Imperial Chinese robes. (Other Far Eastern textiles can be seen in Primary Galleries 44 and 47D, devoted to the art of China and Japan.)

Room 97. This room holds the V & A study collection of carpets, and it is the only study room which requires the services of an attendant. Some 400 carpets are hung in a large circular file which is locked when not in use. The pieces are grouped according to

Room 101 in the V & A's Textile Study Rooms. It is devoted to displays of English embroidery, European embroidery, and printed textiles.

origin and date from the 16th to the 19th Century. Carpets are also displayed in several other areas of the museum, principally in Halls 32 and 33, in the stairwells leading up from these two halls, and in the Primary Galleries devoted to Near Eastern, Far Eastern, and Indian art. In addition, the V & A has a reserve collection of about 240 rugs, which can be seen by appointment.

Room 96. This room is not large, but it is packed with rich source material. One half of the room is devoted to lace; the other half, to European peasant work.

The lace exhibit shows some extraordinarily fine examples of both needlepoint and bobbin lace from all the European centers of lacemaking and dating from the 16th to the 19th Century. They are displayed on walls, in glass-topped drawers, and in removable panel frames. Over 300 examples are exposed for careful study.

Peasant work is similarly displayed in the other half of the room. It is dominantly embroidery, especially strong in work from the Greek Islands.

Rooms 95, 94. These last two rooms of the textile study section are devoted to tapestries. Selections are changed from time to time, thus exposing a full range of the V & A holdings.

Indian Section — Students' Room (off Room 28, ground floor). This facility is comparable to the study rooms of the Textile Department, but it can be used only by appointment, since it also serves as the reserve store for the Indian Section.

The Students' Room holds about 3,000 pieces of textile and costume — in cabinets, drawers, and pull-out frames. There are work tables for researchers, and knowledgeable members of the Indian Section staff are available to answer questions and show the collection. Not that this is necessary: everything stored in the room is well organized, with drawers and cabinets clearly labeled by region and category. (Other examples of Indian textile art are in Primary Galleries 41, 47A, and 47B.)

The Print Room (off room 71). The Print Room is the library and study facility for the museum's Department of Prints & Drawings. To textile designers it can be one of the most important rooms at the V & A. As already noted, this department holds a major portion of the 10,000 textile designs on paper. Most of them are informatively listed in the Print Room catalog, and many are described in the departmental "Handbook" (1964).

The Print Room holds designs for woven and printed fabrics, for embroideries, and for lace. They cover a time span from the 17th Century to the present. The most extensive group dates from the 18th and 19th Centuries and is predominantly English in origin. For example, there are many designs for English woven silks made during the first half of the 18th Century — 82 designs from 1717 and 766 designs from that period up to 1756. Many of these are by the Spitalfields designer Anna Maria Garthwaite, and they reveal fashionable patterns of the time.

There are many French textile designs from the middle and late 18th Century and others from 1820–70, including designs for elaborate French shawls, which are conceded to be finer than those made either at Paisley or Norwich.

Designers for the English arts-and-crafts movement (1870–1900) are well represented, including the pioneer work of William Morris.

There are English block impressions from the 1740s and copperplate impressions (over 100) from the Bromley Hall factory, dating from 1760 to 1800.

There are 17th-Century pattern books from Italy, France, and Germany, as well as many European designs for embroidery and lace, including about 50 of the most important lace pattern books from the 16th and 17th Centuries.

Cornuaud Designs. The Print Room also holds about 2,500 hand-painted designs for printed fabrics by the French designer J. D. Cornuaud, who worked in England from about 1845 to 1880. This group of designs calls for a more extensive note in order to correct a long-standing error.

The Eleventh Edition of the Encyclopaedia Britannica (1910–1911) carried an article on "Textile Printing — Art & Archaeology." It was written by Alan Summerly Cole, who, among other works, produced a catalog on the V & A textile collection. Mr. Cole was the son of Sir Henry Cole, first director of the V & A. In his article (Volume 26, page 708) Mr. Cole wrote the following note:

"An interesting series of over 2,500 patterns, chiefly of this character (i.e., adaptations of woven patterns — ed.) was made by M. Corimand between 1846 and 1860 and is preserved in the National Art Library at South Kensington."

This is the V & A library. I was naturally intrigued by the Britannica entry and went hunting, in vain for some time. There was no reference anywhere in the V & A library to a M. Corimand. I then tried the Print Room catalog. Again no luck. I was about to give up the hunt. But half-heartedly continuing to turn the pages of the Print Room catalog under the letter "C," I was rewarded with one of those victories which brighten the day of a researcher.

There it was! Not under "M. Corimand," but under "J. D. Cornuaud." A typesetter had obviously mistranscribed Mr. Cole's handwritten entry, and the error was recorded for posterity.

The catalog listing reads as follows (Cat. no. T96-T120):

"J. D. Cornuaud (worked c. 1840–c. 1880). A collection of original designs, sketches, working drawings, and specimens of materials by J. D. Cornuaud, chiefly of silk

One section of the National Art Library at the V & A. It is considered the largest art reference library in the world, with close to half a million books, pamphlets, and periodicals on both fine and applied art.

fabrics, including 2,459 designs and 1,247 pieces of silk. Acc. no. D. 2158-4614-1900. Given by Mrs. J. D. Cornuaud."

A note adds that Cornuaud was also a shawl designer, a pupil of Jules Meunier at L'Ecole Royal des Beaux Arts de Lyon, and worked in Lyon until about 1845, when he migrated to England and became a designer in Macclesfield.

There are 24 large portfolios of M. Cornuaud's work. His paintings are mounted on 18-by-22-inch boards, two to six on a board, and they offer valuable documentation on the patterns popular during this period both in England and France. Some might consider M. Cornuaud a hack, but I found the designs interesting, varied, and skillfully executed.

The National Art Library. Since some of the textile designs owned by the V & A are divided between the Print Department and the Library (the Cornuaud case is one example), researchers are well advised to check both sources for specific material.

Aside from that, the National Art Library at the V & A is an incredibly rich resource for textile designers, or for any other kind of designer. As already noted, it owns close to half a million books, pamphlets, and periodicals on the arts — both fine and applied — and it is the largest art reference library in the world.

It also owns a vast store of some 200,000 photographs showing art objects in many parts of the world. Unfortunately, these are not housed in the V & A building, but they are cataloged and can be made available on request. They include many source materials of interest to textile designers, such as ironwork, inn signs, architectural decorations, and detail photographs of artifacts displayed at the Great Exhibition of 1851, which was held at the Crystal Palace (destroyed by fire in 1936). The photographic file also has a number of pictures showing specific ancient textiles held in

such places as the Reims Cathedral and Prague.

Also in the V & A Library is a comprehensive collection of current art periodicals.

V & A Publications on Textiles. In print as of 1974 were the following.

"Basic Stitches of Embroidery" by N. Victoria Wade (28 pages line drawings).

"Batiks" by John Irwin and Veronica Murphy (Three color and 32 large-scale B/W photographs, 8¼ × 11¾, 52 pages, paperback). Good technical and historical explanations.

"Brief Guide to the Costume Court." Small pamphlet, no illustrations.

"Chinese Court Robes in the V & A" by Edmund Capon, Keeper of the Far Eastern Section (V & A Bulletin reprint).

"Collingwood-Coper." Rugs and wall hangings by Peter Collingwood, pots by Hans Coper.

"The Devonshire Hunting Tapestries" by George Wingfield Digby. The famous V & A tapestries discussed by the former Keeper of the V & A Textile Department.

"Elizabethan Embroidery." Small picture book with 27 photographs and technical notes.

"English Chintz." Small picture book with 32 photographs and notes.

"English Printed Textiles." Large picture book with short introduction, 64 B/W photographs, and detailed descriptions of fabrics.

"The Fashionable Lady of the 19th Century" by C. H. Gibbs-Smith, Keeper Emeritus of the National Art Library. A pictorial survey with over 200 illustrations.

"Fifty Masterpieces of Textiles." Fifty small photographs with illuminating notes.

"Flowers in English Embroidery." Small picture book with 27 photographs and technical notes.

"Gospel Stories in English Embroidery." Picture book with 32 photographs.

"Guide to English Embroidery" by Patricia Wardle. Excellent historical introduction, 93 B/W photographs, well reproduced.

"Notes on Applied Work & Patchwork" (17 photos with historical notes).

"Notes on Carpet-Knotting & Weaving." Illustrations and notes.

"Notes on Quilting." (17 photos with historical notes).

"Origins of Chintz" by John Irwin and Katharine B. Brett. Mr. Irwin is Keeper of the Indian Section at the V & A. Mrs. Brett is Curator of Textiles at the Royal Ontario Museum in Toronto. This is a fascinating and definitive work on this subject, with numerous photographs of chintz from the collections at the two museums.

"Samplers" by Donald King, Keeper, Textile Department, V & A. Large picture-book format.

"Shawls" by John Irwin. Monograph with 53 photographs.

"A Venetian Embroidered Altar Frontal" by Donald King (V & A Bulletin reprint).

On Xerox or microfilm only: "Catalogue of Early Mediaeval Woven Fabrics" (1925), "Catalogue of Muhammedan Textiles of the Mediaeval Period" (1924), both by A. F. Kendrick.

Postcards. A large number of postcards — in both color and B/W — show representative pieces in the textile collections.

Home of The Whitworth Art Gallery at the University of Manchester. It is one of the U.K.'s most important facilities for the study of textiles.

MANCHESTER

The Gallery of English Costume
See listing after Whitworth Gallery

MANCHESTER

The Whitworth Art Gallery
University of Manchester M15 6ER
TEL: (061) 273-1880

Joan Allgrove, Keeper of Textiles

The Whitworth Art Gallery ranks next to the V & A in the importance and range of its textile holdings as well as in its facilities for research. It has been part of Manchester University since 1958 and naturally benefits from an association with one of Britain's major educational institutions. Its location is also fortuitous. It is pleasantly situated next to the University's green grounds and is easily reached from the city center by the 123 bus.

It holds at least 11,000 pieces of historic fabric and costume, plus a wallpaper collection of about 1,000 pieces. The total may be even larger, since not all accessions have been cataloged, and an early system of listings often grouped a number of unrelated pieces on one accession card.

Recently the museum completed a major modernization program on its building, and the textile department is now one of the chief beneficiaries of these new installations.

Facilities for the display and study of textiles are most impressive. One large gallery, Darbishire Hall, is devoted to changing exhibits of fabrics. The museum's textile study room is large and comfortable. Representative pieces from the collection are stored here, they are easily accessible, and catalog information is well organized. Nearby is a newly constructed textile conservation room.

The study room holds a small but carefully selected library of works on textile design and history, as well as a large number of textile exhibition catalogs from museums around the world. It is also able to tap the much larger resources of the University art library and the holdings of the Manchester Museum, which is part of the university complex.

A Study Collection

Most important of all, the museum makes every possible effort to have the collection accessible to researchers — something that, unfortunately, cannot be said for most museums. Obviously this is museum policy at the Whitworth, but it also reflects the energetic personality of Joan Allgrove, its knowledgeable and resourceful keeper of textiles.

In short, the Whitworth Gallery is one of the U. K.'s most important resources for all designers and students of the textile art. This is as it should be, since Manchester is the center of Lancashire's great textile industry, and there are a number of textile colleges in the region. Students of these smaller colleges as well as those at the University are encouraged to take advantage of the Whitworth's collections and study facilities. The museum views its holdings as a study collection to be used for education and inspiration.

I find this attitude admirable and refreshing — in sad contrast to the many museums who seem to regard themselves as mere repositories and make it difficult for researchers and designers to explore their holdings.

This laudable policy was, in fact, basic to the aims of the museum founders. When it was opened in 1899, the intent was to establish a museum devoted to the industrial arts — with particular attention to the cotton textile industry, which was then the economic base of the region. The Gallery was named after Sir Joseph Whitworth (1803–1887), a Manchester engineer and industrialist who was responsible (among other things) for the world-wide adoption of uniform screw threads. The man chiefly instrumental in founding the museum, however, was Robert D. Darbishire, a friend and legatee of Joseph Whitworth. The long textile gallery is named after him.

Early Acquisitions

The aims of the founding committee (which included textile producers) was later broadened, but the interest in historic textiles remained strong. Among the first acquisitions was an important collection of ancient European textiles dating from the 15th to the 19th Century. It was assembled by Sir Charles Robinson, a diplomat who served in the Middle East and the Mediterranean.

Another early acquisition was a major collection of Coptic textiles given to the museum by Sir William Flinders Petrie, the archaeologist who excavated burying grounds at Akhmin in Egypt.

Modern Textile Design

These impressive early acquisitions became the foundation of today's large textile holdings at the Whitworth. They were later built up through purchases and through gifts such as the Newberry collection of embroideries from the Near East and the Mediterranean. The latter came to the museum in 1949. Another facet of the Whitworth's holdings which should interest textile designers is the collection of about 1,000 wallpapers acquired in 1967. They were presented to the museum by the Wallpaper Manufacturers Ltd. after the Wallpaper Museum in London was discontinued.

Today, the textile department at the Whitworth is actively engaged in collecting not only ancient textiles but also contemporary fabrics of many types, which are

Darbishire Hall at the Whitworth Art Gallery, recently modernized, and devoted to changing exhibits of historic and modern textiles in the collection.

displayed in annual exhibits that form a record of textile-design trends in the 20th Century.

This acquisition of contemporary fabrics takes ingenious forms. For example, Mrs. Allgrove is currently collecting men's neckwear of the recent past. She has been cutting up the neckwear and arranging the pieces in chronological sequence — in much the same way as 19th-Century Japanese collectors preserved pieces of the superb Japanese silks which were woven for court robes.

Unfortunately, few textile collections have taken the trouble to acquire such contemporary fabrics, and unless the Whitworth's example is followed by others, the record of 20th-Century textile design will be very slim in the years to come.

Further details on the main textile groupings in the Whitworth collection are listed below.

European Woven Silks. This group numbers over 1,000 pieces and is the largest single entity in the holdings. It includes many of the fabrics assembled by Sir Charles Robinson. There is a wide range of silk damasks, brocatelles, brocades, and satins, chiefly from Italy and France, dating from the 15th to the 19th Century. One of the oldest pieces is a 15th-Century Rhenish altar frontal from Germany. It depicts the Tree of Jesse in tapestry weave.

European Velvets. An exceptionally large group for a collection of early velvets. There are some 500 pieces, chiefly from the great weaving cities of Italy during the 16th and 17th Centuries.

European Prints. This is a smaller group of about 200 pieces, representing a wide range of fabric designs printed in Continental Europe beginning in the 17th Century. Prints from Germany and France are the dominant groups, and there is a good representation of 18th-Century Toiles de Jouy.

European Embroidery and Lace. About 200 pieces of secular work and 300 pieces of ecclesiastical embroidery are held in this group, as well as over 500 pieces of lace. The lace work comes from both Continental Europe and the British Isles and represents a full range of types and periods.

Great Britain. British textiles — printed, woven, and embroidered — are represented by at least 1,150 pieces. Some 600 are prints, 350 are wovens, and 200 are embroideries. They cover a wide time span from the mid-18th Century to the present, but the greatest concentration is in 19th-Century prints, particularly those of the English craft-revival movement spearheaded by William Morris. Among these is a group of pattern books from the firm of Bernard Wardle, showing experimental printing of Morris designs between 1875 and 1896. The museum also has a large group of other fabrics from this period, with designs by Morris, Lewis F. Day, Lindsay Butterfield, and C. A. Voysey, as well as a pair of Morris tapestries with figures by Burne-Jones.

Among the earlier pieces in the British group is the now-famous embroidered casket made by 12-year-old Hannah Smith in 1656; also, a 15th-Century embroidered chasuble.

Among the later pieces are many modern home-furnishings fabrics, both printed and woven, dating from the 1950s onwards. Among the chief contributors to these holdings have been such trend-setting forms as Heal's, Hull Traders, and Edinburgh Weavers. These contemporary fabrics, as already noted, are the themes of annual exhibits at the Whitworth and are therefore increasing in number year by year.

Middle East & Mediterranean. This is another major category in the collection, numbering some 700 pieces. It includes wovens, prints, and embroidered fabrics, as well as rugs. Among them are the

embroideries presented to the Whitworth in 1949 by Professor and Mrs. P. E. Newberry. Some date from as early as the 17th Century, and two of the most important segments contain extremely fine examples of Turkish and Greek work. There are also excellent examples of embroidery from Persia, Bokhara, Algeria, and Morocco.

Egypt. This is a most important and representative collection of early Egyptian textiles, expanded from the nucleus of Coptic fabrics given to the museum by Sir William Flinders Petrie. It now numbers over 600 pieces, dating from the 4th to the 11th Century. In addition to the Coptic pieces, the group now includes later acquisitions of Graeco-Roman and early Islamic textiles. The museum is fortunate in owning several complete early Egyptian garments with clave decorations in tapestry weave. There are also early silks from Persia, Syria, and Mesopotamia, as well as from Egypt.

Far East. The Whitworth now owns some 450 pieces of textiles and costumes from China, Japan, and India. They include a number of traditional embroidered court robes, some fine examples of brocaded satin, and palampores in the painted-and-dyed technique from 17th-Century India.

Eastern Europe. From the Balkans and other neighboring regions the Whitworth holds a group of some 350 pieces. They include both woven and embroidered fabrics, chiefly dating from the 19th Century.

Latin America. This is a small group of about 120 pieces. The majority are ethnographic fabrics and costumes. They also include the beginning of an ancient Peruvian collection and a number of pieces from Mexico and Guatemala, which came from the McDougall collection.

The Wallpaper Collection. In 1967, after the British Wallpaper Manufacturers Lim-

Whitworth Gallery Cont'd

ited discontinued the Wallpaper Museum in London, its collection of ancient and modern wallpapers was presented to the Whitworth. In all, the collection consists of about 1,000 pieces. Of these, only about 300 of the more historic papers have been cataloged. Some of them date from the 16th and 17th Centuries. The rest are principally 20th-Century papers and designs, which have not yet been carefully examined. However, they are available to researchers on request, and all the papers should be of interest to textile designers. This collection is under the supervision of Christopher J. Allan, the Assistant Keeper of Prints. A set of 20 color slides is available, showing historic wallpapers dating from 1509 to 1881.

The above listings represent the major cataloged groupings of textiles held by the Whitworth, but they do not by any means reveal all the museum's holdings — as explained earlier. Reserve stores are still in the process of being cataloged, but they are nevertheless accessible to interested researchers. Among the latter are recently acquired ethnographic materials and a group of 20th-Century Turcoman pieces from Northern Iran, which includes weaving, embroidery, and rugs.

Publications Museum publications related to textiles include "A Short Guide to the Whitworth Art Gallery" (1968), five postcards of textiles in color, and five exhibition catalogs. The catalogs are:

"Modern Art in Textile Design" (1962).

"Textiles S.I.A." (1963). Contemporary fabrics designed by members of the Society of Industrial Artists.

"Brown/Craven/Dodd" (1965). Contemporary fabrics by three designers — Barbara Brown, Shirley Craven, and Robert Dodd.

"British Sources of Art Nouveau" (1969). Nineteenth-Century textiles, wallpapers, furniture, etc., chiefly from the Whitworth collections.

"The Turcoman of Iran" (1971). An exhibit jointly produced with the Abbot Hall Art Gallery, Kendal.

MANCHESTER

The Gallery of English Costume
Platt Hall, Rusholme M14 5LL
TEL: (061) 224-5217

Christina Hawkins, Keeper
Mary Davey, Asst. Keeper

A 15-minute walk from the Whitworth Gallery brings you to the well-known Gallery of English Costume, administered by the City of Manchester Art Galleries. It is well worth a visit.

Though not properly a textile collection, it warrants brief mention here for several reasons.

1. It holds some 4,000 costumes and about 2,000 accessories which illustrate the trends in British apparel fabrics, chiefly for women, from 1760 to the present.

2. It has a good collection of embroidery and a modest one of lace.

3. It owns a number of valuable fabric sample books.

Some additional comments can be made on each of these counts.

Costume Collection. For textile designers the displays at Platt Hall are often interestingly related to the textiles used. An example of this is a display of Victorian costume which also contains a pattern book of Victorian dress fabrics. A printed caption to the exhibit explains that wools and cottons of the 1830s were muted in color because of the limited shades available from vegetable dyes. These gave way to richer colors on figured silks in the 1850s.

By the 1860s, aniline dyes were in wide use and this resulted in bolder colors for cottons and wools, usually taking the design form of strong stripes and checks. Some of these fabrics are shown in the fabric sample book on display with the costumes.

Other exhibits in the museum reveal similar connections of interest to the textile designer and student. There is also an extensive library with early fashion plates, which will reveal further connections.

Lace and Embroidery. Apart from lace and embroidery integral to costumes, the Gallery also owns some 200 pieces of separate lacework and at least 1,000 pieces of embroidery. Moreover, the work is not only English. It was collected before the museum began to specialize in English costume.

Among the embroideries are fine pieces from China, Japan, India, Egypt, Persia, Greece, Turkey, and most countries in Europe. They may eventually be transferred to other collections, but at this writing they are held by the Gallery and form an interesting resource for designers. The museum also owns close to a dozen patchwork quilts.

Sample Books. Somewhat neglected in the Gallery — but no less valuable — is a quite substantial collection of fabric sample books and unmounted swatches. There are eight large, bound volumes of printed fabric samples which formerly belonged to the Rossendale collection. They cover eight separate periods between 1808 and 1852 and thus form a valuable record of print-design trends during those years. There are also 17 large boxes of unmounted fabric samples, which include both apparel and household textiles.

The Gallery of English Costume is therefore a useful resource for textile designers. Its close proximity to the Whitworth should offer added inducement for a visit to this red-brick, Georgian mansion set in a pleasant, flower-bordered park.

Two views of the Strangers' Hall Museum, Norwich. Part of the building dates from the year 1320. It houses some 20 period rooms furnished in different styles of English decor from the early 16th to the late 19th Century.

Publications. The Gallery has published nine small picture booklets dealing with different periods of English costume in chronological sequence. They cover the following subjects.

1. "A Brief View." Capsule survey, 1770–1937.
2. "18th Century." Women's costume.
3. "1800 to 1835." Women's costume.
4. "1835 to 1870." Women's costume.
5. "1870 to 1900." Women's costume.
6. "1900 to 1930." Women's costume.
7. "Children's Costume."
8. "Women's Costume for Sport."
9. "Fashion in Miniature."

Each booklet contains 20 pages of illustrations, showing costumes and accessories photographed on live models. Each has a short introduction and good descriptive captions.

Postcards. In addition, the Gallery issues eight B/W and six color postcards, as well as 13 color transparencies.

NEWCASTLE-UPON-TYNE

Laing Art Gallery & Museum
Higham Pl. NE1 8AG
TEL: Newcastle 26989

Margaret Gill, Keeper, Applied Arts

The Laing Gallery owns only a small group of textiles, but it is notable for the fine Bosanquet collection of Mediterranean embroideries, which it shares with Newcastle University.

Between the two holdings there are about 75 pieces, chiefly from the Greek Islands but also from northern Greece, Morocco, Spain, Italy, Sicily, Turkey, and Albania. The work dates from the 17th to the 19th Century and includes some rare examples. Most of it was collected at the turn of the century by Professor Robert Carr Bosanquet, who was then Director of the School of Archaeology in Athens.

In addition to embroideries, the Laing Gallery owns seven pieces of well-preserved Coptic tapestry weaving of the 4th to the 9th Century, about a dozen 18th-Century English brocades, a similar number of ecclesiastical embroideries of the 16th and 18th Centuries, and a group of 30 English samplers dating from the 17th to the 19th Century.

The museum also collects English costume and owns a number of ensembles dating from the 18th to the 20th Century.

NORWICH

Strangers' Hall Museum
Charing Cross N0R 65B
TEL: (0603) 22233 Ext 645

Bridget Yates, Keeper, Social History
Fiona Strodder, Asst. Keeper

Norwich, like Paisley, was an important production center for shawls throughout the first half of the 19th Century. Shawls produced in the two towns were indistinguishable, and they competed with each other in both domestic and foreign markets.

Norwich shawls actually came first, but by the 1860s Paisley had taken the lead, outproducing and underselling its competitors — which also included Edinburgh. So much so that eventually the term "Norwich Shawl" fell into disuse and was forgotten. Today it is hardly known, and the term "Paisley Shawl" has become generic. (Further details on Paisley shawls will be found in the review of the Paisley Museum.)

The term "Paisley" is now frequently used loosely to describe a large shawl, woven by machine, with a "pine" motif in imitation of handmade shawls from Kashmir. The latter were imported into Europe by the East India Companies and were in vogue at least by 1770.

The Norwich Shawl Industry

Norwich was well established as a textile center, turning out woven and printed fabrics long before it began to produce shawls. Its first successful imitation of a Kashmir shawl was made in 1792 by John Harvey and P. J. Knights. It was constructed with a silk warp and a wool weft. The decorative motifs were embroidered by hand in a darning stitch.

By 1812, there were 12 shawl producers in Norwich, and decorations were still embroidered by hand. But shortly thereafter a technique was evolved for making the complete shawl, including decorations, on a draw loom. The shawls were generally 45 or 54 inches wide, sometimes square in shape but also up to 2½ yards long.

By 1830, the jacquard loom began to take over, and by 1843, at least 26 shawl manufacturers were using it in Norwich.

Long before that, Norwich mills were also producing printed versions of the Kashmir shawl. They were considered "poor relations" of the machine-woven shawl and were therefore cheaper in price, though not necessarily less beautiful. The printed versions are very intricate in design and often quite luxurious to modern eyes. This is particularly true of the summer shawls, printed on silk leno weaves with a stabilizing band of tighter weaving—about two inches wide—at each end.

The high point of shawl manufacturing in Norwich was reached from the 1840s through the 1850s. There were 28 manufacturers in the industry and one of them, E. & F. Hinde, recorded for the year 1849 a production of 39,000 shawls in 26 different designs. Some were as large as four by two yards, and one type was a reversible pattern patented by W. H. Clabburn in 1854.

Strangers' Hall Museum

All these types of shawls and many more are now held by the Strangers' Hall

FAR LEFT. Detail of a woven shawl by Willet & Co., Norwich, c. 1850.

LEFT. Detail of printed leno shawl by Towler & Campin, Norwich, c. 1850.

BELOW. Pattern for a woven shawl by Willet & Co. of Norwich.

All from Strangers' Hall Museum.

Strangers' Hall
Museum Cont'd

Museum in Norwich. The museum is housed in an ancient and quite fascinating building. Part of it dates from the year 1320 and other sections were added through the 15th, 16th, and 17th Centuries. It is thus a living relic of Britain's past, with some 20 rooms furnished in period styles ranging from the early 16th to the late 19th Century.

Nor is Strangers' Hall the only reason to visit Norwich. The town's Castle Museum dominates the city center from its fortified hilltop site. It holds some textiles but is better known for its collections of art (including art of the Norwich School), local archaeology, and natural history. Another attraction is the Bridewell Museum, devoted to local industries and rural crafts, including the shawl industry. Norwich also has one of Britain's great cathedrals and an ancient market square which is still used for that purpose. It is a very pleasant town for a day's excursion from London, rewarding the visitor with a quality of life which echoes England's past far more than most cities in the U.K. today.

The Shawl Collection

For textile designers and students, however, the collections at Strangers' Hall Museum will be the chief attraction. The museum owns over 300 shawls, representing all types produced in Norwich. It also owns photostatic copies of all Norwich design registrations entered in the Patent Office from 1842 onward. In addition, it has a collection of some 300 photographs showing designs from the pattern books of rival Paisley.

Aside from shawls, Strangers' Hall holds a large and interesting collection of occupational and religious dress. It numbers over 8,000 pieces and is chiefly 20th-Century material, with a few pieces from the 19th Century. Added to this is a

substantial group of domestic furnishings with an emphasis on 19th-Century wool work. In this category are 65 decorative bed coverings, dating from 1700 to 1960, including 29 patchwork quilts.

Three other segments of the textile collection are worthy of mention.

1. Lace and Embroidery. The lace group is modest, but the embroidery group is large, and most of it relates either to costume or domestic furnishings.

2. Samplers. There are 122 pieces in this group, and they date from the 17th to the 20th Century. Most are of English origin.

3. Pattern Books. This collection reflects the long history of Norwich as a textile-producing center. There are about 50 pattern and order books from a number of Norwich firms, and they show both woven and printed fabrics made between 1759 and 1880.

Publication. "Norwich Shawls." A booklet on the history of the shawl industry in Norwich, illustrated with photographs of representative shawls from the Strangers' Hall collection.

NOTTINGHAM
Castle Museum & Art Gallery
The Castle NG1 6EL
TEL: (0602) 43615

Jeremy W. Farrell, Keeper of Textiles

Since Nottingham was and continues to be a center of lacemaking, its museum logically concentrates on this branch of the textile arts. The collection is large and varied.

The museum owns about 2,000 pieces of both handmade and machine-made lace. The handmade pieces date from the 16th Century to the present, covering most of the traditional sources and periods both in the U.K. and foreign countries. Lace tools and pattern books are included in the collection.

Machine-made lace held by the museum dates from about 1760 onward. It reflects the many different constructions and types which were adapted for machine production. It shows work made on Vickers and Leavers machines in many styles and for many uses.

In addition to its lace collection, the Castle Museum holds six other categories of textiles which are worthy of mention.

1. Costume. About 2,000 items dating from the 17th Century to modern times. Its best representation begins in 1820.

2. Woven and Printed. About 100 pieces of woven and printed fabrics from the 18th Century and forward. These are both dress and home-furnishing fabrics.

3. Embroidery. About 150 pieces, including a number of samplers, bedspreads, and curtains. The earliest pieces are from the 16th Century.

4. Asiatic. A group of about 250 pieces, including embroidered robes and hangings from China and Japan as well as other flat textiles and costumes from India, Persia, Turkey, and the U.S.S.R.

RIGHT. Point net with hand-run pattern, late 18th to early 19th Century.

FAR RIGHT. Velvet lace made on a warp machine, 1855–65.

Both from Nottingham Castle Museum.

5. English. About 50 pieces in the Middleton Collection of English Costume & Embroidery. It includes very rare examples of 16th- to 18th-Century work.

6. Dolls. About 40 dolls and dolls' clothing from various periods.

All parts of the collection can be seen by appointment. At this writing, however, research facilities are limited. A move to larger quarters has been planned, and when this occurs, study rooms will be set aside for textile research.

Industrial Museum. Recently established in Nottingham is a new museum which should interest students and designers of lace. It is the Industrial Museum at Wollaston Hall Stables, and it has a special section devoted to lacemaking.

Early 17th Century gloves with gauntlets embroidered in silk and metal thread. *Nottingham Castle Museum — No. 16.*

OXFORD

The Ashmolean Museum
Beaumont St. OX1 2PH
TEL: (0865) 57522
David Piper, Director

The Ashmolean is, of course, one of Britain's major museums, but textiles play only a minor role in its operation. There is no textile department as such, and no curator is specifically responsible for ancient fabrics. This makes research somewhat difficult, but a little persistence can prove most rewarding.

Specifically, ancient textiles of considerable interest to designers and students are held by three departments at the museum.

1. Western Art Department (H. J. Garlick, Keeper). This is a small group of only 36 pieces, but among them are some fine examples of Opus Anglicanum embroidery from the year 1500 A.D. Several of these are displayed in the public galleries. In all, this department owns about 20 examples of 16th- and 17th-Century needlework, six medieval embroideries, and five tapestries which are on permanent exhibition.

2. Eastern Art Department (Ms. M. Tregear, Senior Asst. Keeper; James Allen, Assistant). This department holds a considerably larger textile collection of over 300 pieces and is wide-ranging in character.

Notable here is a group of about 50 painted hangings (tankas) from Tibet — a remarkable and important collection in itself. Another smaller group consists of embroidered hangings from Burma. I was especially fascinated by one panel with raised embroidery which uses pieces of hammered metal to simulate the scales of fish and the shells of turtles. The collection also includes good examples of textile art from China, Japan, India, and the Greek Islands. There are printed palampores, resist-dyed cottons, woven sashes, and a large number of embroidered silks. In the whole group the strongest representation is from Burma.

All pieces in the collection can be examined in the Seminar Room by appointment.

3. Antiquities Department (H. J. Case, Keeper; P. R. S. Moorey, Senior Asst. Keeper). The largest and most important group of textiles in the museum is held by this department. Most of the pieces are Egyptian in origin, and the largest number were given to the museum by Professor P. E. Newberry, an Egyptologist who taught at the Universities of Liverpool and Cairo. (Other parts of his extensive textile col-

lections went to the Whitworth Gallery in Manchester.)

The Newberry Collection consists of 800 Coptic pieces and 2,000 printed Islamic textiles — all from Egypt.

The Coptic fragments cover a long time span — from about the 4th Century onward. All pieces are mounted and carefully cataloged in a typescript book of 293 large foolscap pages.

Some of the earliest Coptic pieces are easily examined, since they are displayed in the Egyptian gallery on both sides of eight hinged panels. Most of these date from the 4th to the 7th Century, but one piece is far more ancient. It dates from about 1900 B.C. and is therefore one of the most ancient patterned textiles held by any museum. The display of this piece is accompanied by a graphic chart showing how it was constructed.

Another interesting display in the same exhibit shows a weaving kit of colored wools and reed needles found in a tomb at Hawara. It dates from the 4th Century A.D.

The printed Islamic textiles are more difficult to study, since they are stored in a large cabinet standing at the center of a public exhibition gallery. They consist of both larger pieces and fragments. Those I examined seemed to be printed by a stamping process, though I cannot be sure. The museum dates these printed textiles from the 8th Century onwards, with many falling into the 13th and 14th Centuries. Further research is obviously needed on this large and valuable collection.

In addition to these two major groupings, the Antiquities Department also owns smaller collections of Roman and Anglo-Saxon fabrics from England, some Neolithic textiles of the Swiss Lake Dwellers, and a number of rare pieces from Nymphaeum in the Crimea, dated in the 5th Century B.C.

Brilliantly colored Hawaiian feather cape from the ethnographic collections at the *Pitt Rivers Museum, Oxford.*

OXFORD

Pitt Rivers Museum
Parks Rd. OX1 3PP
TEL: (0865) 54979

Donald B. Taylor, Asst. Curator

Perhaps the most exciting feature of the Pitt Rivers Museum is its approach through the Oxford University Museum. You find yourself in a great hall under a roof of vaulted Gothic arches — but the arches are filled with glass and the light pours in through a fretwork of structural iron. This combination of bright skylight and intricate Gothic arches is a brilliant aesthetic concept, but it also serves the very functional purpose of bathing the displays in clear daylight.

The large ethnographical collection of textiles held by Pitt Rivers was not easy to explore during my visit, since the reserve stores were not accessible due to an extensive reorganization program then underway. However, a good deal of the material was on exhibit in the galleries, and much of what I saw was both rare and interestingly displayed.

Exhibits by Type

The arrangement of exhibits in this museum is different than that in many other museums, and the principle behind the arrangement seems most valid to me. It is based on the policy of Lt. Gen. Pitt Rivers, founder of the museum, who believed that all artifacts should be displayed by typology rather than by geographic or cultural origin. That means, for example, that all textiles and textile tools of a similar type should be displayed together, even though they come from widely separated regions of the world.

The result is a series of exhibits which forces the viewer to make connections and comparisons. For example, a large exhibit of tapa cloths is drawn from widely dispersed cultures. It is the best display of tapa I have yet seen in any museum, showing pieces from Micronesia, Australia, Africa, South America, Hawaii, Melanesia, and Indonesia. The range of patterns is wide, revealing many different styles which would be most stimulating to a contemporary textile designer.

Another informative exhibit displays and describes a large group of primitive looms from the following regions: Malay Archipelago, Formosa, Borneo, Assam, Burma, East Asia, South Nigeria, Santa Cruz, the Caroline Islands, West Africa, America (Hopi Indians), and Norway (Lapps).

Other exhibits contain Eskimo beadwork, painted deerskins of the Cherokee Indians, and a wide range of textiles from Dyak (ikat), ancient Peru, Sarawak, Ghana (Ashanti weaving), the Canadian Indians (beadwork), and the Caroline Islands. The last group has interesting patterned weavings made from banana fiber.

A special exhibit is devoted to the textiles and weaving techniques of village craftsmen in the Andes Mountains and was based on an expedition sponsored by the museum. And the most dramatic display of all shows a great crescent-shaped feather cloak made in the Hawaiian Islands about 1840.

Rare Acquisitions

Aside from these exhibits, the museum staff informs me that Pitt Rivers owns a rare collection of embroidery made with hair — including pieces from Siberia and North America. They also hold textiles of grass fiber from Sierre Leone, decorated cottons from Southeast Asia, and a large group of fabrics from Guatemala and Mexico, which were acquired from the McDougall Collection.

Altogether a most stimulating source of ethnographic textiles.

The Pitt Rivers Museum is attached to the Department of Ethnology and Prehistory at Oxford University. It is open to the public on weekdays only from 2–4 P.M.

Publications. Two publications on the collection have been issued by the Oxford University Press.

"The McDougall Collection of Indian Textiles from Guatemala and Mexico" by Laura E. Start (with 100 line drawings by the author).

"Hair Embroidery in Siberia and North America" by Geoffrey Turner (illustrated with photographs).

PAISLEY

Museum & Art Galleries
High St. PA1 2BA
TEL: (041) 889-3151

James Hunter, Keeper of Textiles

The alphabetical arrangement in this book puts Norwich before Paisley, and while Norwich is nearer to London, the textile collection at Paisley is the more important resource for research into shawl design — as it was for the shawls themselves in the 19th Century. Designers will find a visit to Paisley very rewarding, and it is only 20 minutes by public transportation (Bus 15) from the Kelvingrove Museum in Glasgow.

The Paisley Shawl Industry

The shawl industry operated successfully in Paisley — with ups and downs — from 1805 into the early 1870s. It was begun by an Edinburgh textile manufacturer who found skilled (and cheap) weaving labor in nearby Paisley. The objective — as in Norwich somewhat earlier — was to copy by machine the intricate and expensive shawls from Kashmir, then so popular in Europe.

Typical weaver's cottage of the 18th and early 19th Centuries where Paisley fabrics were woven. Living quarters were on the left, and the weaving shop on the right with a loom at each window. *Museum & Art Galleries, Paisley.*

Long before the advent of shawls, Paisley had specialized in weaving — as far back as the mid-17th Century. It expanded rapidly during the 18th Century, but its boom came through the shawl industry. From 3,600 looms operating in 1792, it jumped to 7,000 looms in 1820 and employed an equal number of weavers.

Almost from the beginning, the aim of the Paisley mills was to cater to a mass market. They did this through cheap labor, careful organization, and ruthless competition, so they were able to outproduce and undersell their competitors in both Edinburgh and Norwich. By the 1840s Edinburgh mills had abandoned the field, and by the 1860s Norwich was a poor second in the trade. Pricing was the key to Paisley's success in the market. From about 1820 to 1850 the average price of a fairly simple shawl in England was between £7 and £10; a more complicated design sold for £20 to £30. Even during that period Norwich mills complained that Paisley was copying their designs at half the price. But by 1860, the Paisley shawl industry was so well rationalized that it was able to sell its products at 17 to 27 shillings apiece. (By comparison, an authentic shawl from Kashmir might fetch as much as £200.) At its highest point the Paisley shawl industry did a volume of one million pounds a year.

Its major rival was Lyon in France, which was competitive in price and which is generally admitted to have produced a finer product — both in quality of fabric and intricacy of design.

The "pine" motif which we now loosely call the "paisley" motif was actually not introduced by Paisley mills until sometime between 1814 and 1818. Because they were complicated to make on a draw loom (the equipment then used), these designs were woven in strips and them sewn onto the borders and ends of a white or colored shawl.

Jacquard looms were not used in Paisley until about 1840, and they revolutionized production, converting shawl making from a cottage industry into a factory system. Aesthetically, the results of jacquard weaving were not always good. It gave the designers almost too much flexibility in both pattern and color, so that later shawl designs often tend to be overcrowded and somewhat garish in shade.

The picture which emerges is that of a modern, aggressive industry, competing sharply for both markets and designs, waging price wars, cutting corners on production — and making fortunes in the process.

But by the early 1870s, all this was over. The long-lasting vogue for shawls finally went out of fashion — together with the crinoline, which gave shawls their valid reason for existence. (The shawl served in place of an outercoat, which was difficult to tailor to the extravagant shape of the crinoline.)

Model of a drawloom — a handloom with overhead harness. Looms of this type were used to make the earlier Paisley shawls. After 1840 the Jacquard loom was introduced and changed the cottage industry into a factory system. *Museum & Art Galleries, Paisley.*

The Shawl Collection

But the record of Paisley's flourishing shawl industry is intact in the Paisley Museum. Its collection of shawls and sample books covers 60 years of operation. There are some 700 shawls in the collection, representing all the many different styles made in Paisley mills. And that means not only the ubiquitous pine patterns but also a wide range of woven and printed designs in many other styles.

All these, together with about 70 design and sample books from Paisley mills, are preserved by the museum and are available to researchers. The museum also displays the three types of loom used in shawl production — hand loom, draw loom, and jacquard loom — as well as a large group of weavers' tools.

Shawl Exhibit

Most important of all to the designer and researcher is a recently installed and permanent exhibit devoted entirely to the Paisley shawl — traditionally called a "plaid" in Scotland. The exhibit is large, well hung, and well lighted. Through some 20 superb examples of the shawl craft with accompanying technical and historical notes, it presents an interesting picture of the industry in all its variety. Many of the shawls are displayed together with the original paper designs from which they were made.

Among the important design types shown in the exhibit are the following:

1. An 1850 hand-embroidered shawl from India — an Amli type. This was the prototype imported product which Paisley mills were attempting to duplicate by machine. It is made up of many separate embroidered pieces sewn together with almost invisible stitches.

2. An 1830 copy of a Cantonese silk crepe shawl, decorated with hand embroidery.

Examples of traditional English smock patterns from the collection at the Museum of English Rural Life.
FAR LEFT. Norfolk pattern — *56/243*.
LEFT. Wiltshire, c. 1882 — *55/121*.
BELOW. Berkshire, 1880. — *55/125*.
BOTTOM. Sussex, c. 1880 — *55/124*.

Paisley Museum Cont'd

3. A "White" shawl of 1839, with borders woven separately and sewn on.

4. A "Blue Style" shawl, very popular around 1845–50. Decorations are in blue only, on a white ground.

5. A "Chinese Fairy Tale" shawl of about 1855. It was probably woven in Lyon, France. It is extremely complicated in design, containing human figures and showing no repeat, though it is large. The construction is also remarkably fine, containing 4,000 warp threads in its 37-inch width and 150,000 weft threads.

6. A "Thibet" shawl, made at Paisley in 1857. This style was an attempt to simulate the hand and texture of Kashmir goat's wool through a mixture of silk and wool.

7. A "Compartment" shawl made up with four differently colored background rectangles in the center. It is 11 by 5½ feet in size.

8. A "Zebra" shawl made about 1867. This was derived from the traditional striped weaves of Turkey and was popular during the 1860s.

9. A reversible shawl, which was introduced at Paisley about 1865.

In addition to the shawls themselves, the exhibit shows and explains the complicated process required to translate a paper design into fabric through enlargement and graphing on point paper.

Other Fabrics. Aside from the shawls, the Paisley Museum owns a smaller collection of textile samples showing other types of fabrics made by the local industry. They are mainly muslins and gauzes, and they cover a period from about 1800 to 1830. Some of these examples are also on exhibit.

Publication. "Paisley Shawls" by C. H. Rock, 1966. An illustrated 24-page booklet (8 x 10), with an excellent historical review of the industry and 17 clear photographs of Paisley designs and equipment.

READING

Museum of English Rural Life
University of Reading
Whiteknights RG6 2AG
TEL: (0734) 85123 Ext. 475

Laurel C. Ball, Assistant Keeper

The Museum of English Rural Life was established in 1951 to document the agricultural life of Great Britain. It is attached

to the University of Reading, which is well known for its Faculty of Agriculture. As such, the museum has only a secondary interest in textiles, and it holds a small collection of about 200 pieces, most of them garments.

Smocking Patterns

However, among the costumes is a notable collection of about 40 traditional English smocks, whose pattern work should be of interest to designers and students.

The English smock was a typical work garment worn by men in many agricultural counties of England and Wales. It was a shirtlike garment, generally closed at the front and pulled over the head. It was cut square and very roomy to allow for freedom of movement. Shape was introduced through extensive gathering of the fabric (smocking) at the top of the garment in both front and back.

The smocking became decorative and symbolic around the middle of the 18th Century, though less decorated smocks were worn by workmen in Shakespeare's time. Smocks continued to be worn in English rural areas until about 1880.

The smocking patterns were quite varied and generally symbolized the trade or occupation of the wearer. For example, there were basic traditional designs for such trades as woodsman, carter, butcher, milkmaid, shepherd, gardener, gravedigger, etc. Often, too, different counties had their own regional patterns, as well as special colors in both fabric and thread. (An interesting parallel could perhaps be drawn between these English smocks and the tapestry-decorated shirtlike garments of the ancient Egyptian Copts.)

The Reading Museum of English Rural Life, as noted, owns about 40 of these work garments, and they represent the pattern work of many rural counties. A catalog of the smocks is now in preparation.

A HISTORY OF
BRITISH TEXTILE DESIGN

Of the four basic textile fibres, wool, linen, cotton, and silk, the climate of the British Isles favoured only the first two. From an early period different breeds of sheep were reared and their wool graded and exported before large-scale industries were established. Linen was a localised industry about whose beginnings we know very little. There are few environments which favour the preservation of archeological textiles, least of all in Great Britain. This factor, coupled with the depredation of the common clothes moth and the need of the poor to clothe themselves, albeit in rags, has led to the virtual disappearance of any material evidence of the enormously important English medieval woollen industry. The Lord Chancellor sits on a woolsack, East Anglia has a series of fine churches built as a result of the prosperity of 15th-century clothiers, and many of the livery companies of the City of London (which are now associations of businessmen of many trades) were incorporated to represent the interests of various long-established textile trades: the Worshipful Companies of Drapers (1364), Dyers (1470), Merchant Taylors (1327), Mercers (1393–4), Weavers (1155), for example. These are the major indications of the medieval textile industries outside the manuscripts in every record office of the United Kingdom.

The social and political effects of this industry were far-reaching, but we cannot talk about its designs. Money from wool was invested in other enterprises, and a whole range of ancillary industries became very important: dyestuffs, fulling materials, mordants for dyestuffs, for example. The woollen trade also stimulated overseas trade and mercantile organisation. British woollens went from Novgorod to the Levant and to every part of Europe, spurred by competition at first from the Low Countries and then from France.

Decorated Fabrics

Cotton was not imported into Great Britain before the 16th century, but silks from the Near East, Southern Europe, and Northern Italy were imported at great expense even in the Dark Ages for an exclusive market both secular and ecclesiastical. The relics of St Cuthbert, who died in 687 A.D., include some very important silks from the Near East, now in Durham Cathedral. Sewing and embroidery silk was also imported (though ordinary garments were probably sewn with linen thread). Silk thread was used for some of the finest embroidery ever made: *Opus Anglicanum* was celebrated throughout Europe from the 12th–15th centuries, as we know from references in inventories and the few fortunate survivals from this period. The Bayeux tapestry is perhaps French. There are, however, early English embroideries in which the unfolding of the Gothic style can be discerned as clearly as in contemporary sculpture or illuminated manuscripts. The embroidery of the Syon Cope epitomises the delicacy of the drawing and the artistry of the composition (pages 110–111). The technique of underside couching (see Fig. 1) was one not generally used abroad, and it partly accounts for the texture and quality achieved. Only in the 16th century did *Opus Anglicanum* degenerate from an art to a highly decorative craft (Fig. 2). The cherubim became stereotyped, the stitches coarser. By then, however, a new school of English secular embroidery was emerging.

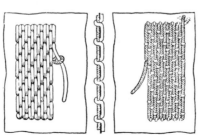

1. Diagram showing the technique of underside couching.

Embroidery — 16th–20th Century

During the 16th–17th century embroidery was both a highly fashionable method of decorating clothes and a way of producing sumptuous furnishings. Gloves and coifs, bodices and doublets, shirts and petticoats were decorated in black silk, red silk, blue silk, gold thread, or many colours, with seed pearls in profusion, as we can see in many contemporary portraits (Fig. 3). Bed hangings and wall coverings might be decorated purely with applied gold or silver braid or with pictorial embroidery of an elaborate symbolism such as the Oxburgh hangings carried out in silk cross-stitch on canvas by Mary Queen of Scots and her gaoler, Bess of Hardwick. During the 17th and early 18th centuries crewelwork hangings for beds (carried out in worsted on a linen and cotton twill) were of great importance (page 8, bottom). Their designs are an amalgam of the ornament on Indian chintzes — itself influenced by the strange flora of European crewelwork. The green has often now faded to blue, for it was a long time before yellow dyes became as fast as other colours, but still crewelwork designs remain fresh and striking. Sheets, pillowcases, cushions, and quilts were finely embroidered, often in monochrome but increasingly in colours. The total effect can be seen in the hangings embroidered by Abigail Pett in the late 17th century, now in the Victoria and Albert Museum. On smaller-scale embroideries stylised floral decoration in detached sprigs is characteristic of the period. Some motifs were passed from embroideress to embroideress; others were taken from printed pattern-books, which were common by the late 16th century, or books of emblems and similar sources. Mirror frames, work boxes, pictures (often with raised embroidery called stumpwork), and samplers show the inventiveness of the craftswoman who began her career as quite a young child. Although samplers were ostensibly in-

tended as a library of embroidery motifs in a repertoire of different stitches, their influence seems to have been more on each other and less on other types of embroidery. Martha Edlin embroidered her coloured sampler (the easiest) in 1668 when she was eight; the next year she did her lace sampler; in 1671 an embroidered casket; and finally, her most difficult task, a beadwork casket, in 1673 (Fig. 4). After the panels of a casket were embroidered, perhaps with some suitable Biblical scene, a local carpenter was employed to mount it.

Domestic embroidery continued, of course, into the 18th and 19th centuries, but it was a tradition of greatly diminished vigour. The Berlin woolwork (page 207) of the 19th century (the name taken from the earliest patterns printed in Berlin) stifled the creative drive of the ordinary embroideress. From then on she came to rely upon a printed pattern with the colours marked out for her and a very limited range of stitches. Dependence on the printed pattern culminated in the modern transfer pattern ironed onto a canvas. Embroideresses of the Arts and Crafts movement, who revolted against the bondage of the commercial pattern, are discussed later in the context of the whole movement.

Schools of professional embroiderers existed from the early Middle Ages onwards. Their daily work was the production of ceremonial and heraldic objects, whose design changed very little, but in the 17th and 18th centuries, especially, such workshops carried out many other commissions. Edmund Harrison, embroiderer to Charles I and later Charles II, was among the most famous, and an occasional example of his work has survived.

Woven Textiles

The story of British textile design as opposed to the history of British textiles begins in the 17th century. From then on

there are fragments, the occasional pattern book of samples, even textiles with a fairly certain British provenance, but there is always the problem of survival. Elaborate and expensive things were the most cherished, and these tended to be the imported silks and not the splendid British woollens. We can form an idea of their appearance by looking at portraits of the time and reading the accounts presented by

3. Dorothy Arundel, wife of Sir Henry Weston, by Zuccaro, early 17th Century. She wears an embroidered English bodice, a robe of Italian silk, and a gauze apron with Italian needlepoint lace and stands on a Turkish carpet placed over rush matting, possibly woven in Norfolk. Paul Getty Collection. *Courtauld Institute — B.64/235.*

the tailor who served James II and William III. No lengths of cloth have survived, but a doll "Lord Clapham" acquired by the V & A in 1974 wears a typical coat (Fig. 5).

Table linen is an exception to the problem of survival. The fibre is tough, durable, and not attractive to moths or other vermin. The earliest table linen for an English customer to have come down to us dates from about 1500 — but it was made in the Low Countries, possibly in Courtrai. Although diapered linen exists, for it was cheaper than damask and much was woven, there is no way of telling whether a diapered cloth is Dutch, Flemish, German, or even British, and it is even difficult to tell whether it dates from the 17th or 19th century. The simple patterns have remained classic designs in the repertoire of hand weavers. In the 18th century, both in Scotland and in Ireland, attempts were successfully made to set up establishments weaving fine-quality table linen (Fig. 6). A feature of the designs of damasks is the use of a point repeat so that the patterns are automatically symmetrical. A napkin (much larger than the present style of table napkin) would have one point repeat, a table cloth several pairs of repeats.

Knitting has been an important technique from the 16th to the 20th century. 16th-century apprentice caps have come to light both in the walls of old buildings and in the mud of the Thames (hurled there by the owner's friends or enemies?); these are plain hand-knitted but styled berets in wool. Hand knitting of a much more elaborate kind survives from the 17th century onwards. It was in England that the Rev. William Lee invented the stocking frame in 1589. British knitting had a high reputation, and silk stockings and other goods were exported.

The distribution of the textile industries in the past was very different from that in the 20th century. Fine, good-quality woollens were made in the West country, not in

5. RIGHT. "Lord Clapham," one of two English dolls, c. 1698–1700. The coat is scarlet cloth. *V &A — GD 4660 (T847–1974).*

6. FAR RIGHT. Scottish napkin, dated 1736 and inscribed "Anna Moray." *V &A — X 22 (T.137–1934).*

Yorkshire. The latter made coarse woollens for blankets and soldiers' clothing well into the 18th century. Norwich was the centre of the fine worsted industry from the 17th century until the late 18th century, and there are pattern books of Norwich worsteds as late as the 1830s (although by then it was making several other important kinds of textile). The best *calimancoes* were exported throughout Europe and to the American colonies in the 18th century. They were not cheap, and their designs in brightly coloured glazed and calendered worsted followed those of contemporary fashionable silks (Fig. 7). Several textile centres in the Midlands were important. Tapestries were woven at Barcheston in Warwickshire in the late 16th century and the first half of the 17th century by the Sheldons, father and son (Fig. 8). Coventry made light worsteds and subsequently ribbons, an industry which became extremely important in the 18th and 19th centuries. The East Midlands, notably Nottingham and Leicester, attracted framework knitters from the 17th century onwards — evading the restrictions of the London guild of framework knitters. They founded the knitting and machine-lace industries which are of such importance today in this area. Above all others, London was possibly the leading textile centre in the country. Not only was London the centre of fashion and of trade with an enormous port, but within London itself and immediately around it were established important textile industries. Sailcloth was made in Southwark and south of the Thames generally, ribbons in the City, as well as worsteds and half silks, gimps and braids, hankerchiefs and gold and silver lace, tapestries and carpets, knitting and ropes, and all the ancillary trades of tailoring and upholstery were practised there. Possibly only broadcloth was not made in London. From the late 17th century textiles were printed just outside London, while the phenomenal growth of the silk industry

along Bishopsgate from the City brought into being a new suburb, Spitalfields. Naturally, these industries varied in size and importance. The royal tapestry works at Mortlake gained European renown — perhaps their most famous set of tapestries being the Acts of the Apostles taken from the cartoons by Raphael. The Vanderbanks produced some highly decorative tapestries in the late 17th and early 18th centuries (Fig. 9), and there were several workshops in Soho, mostly rather short-lived, for their market declined as fashions in wall furnishings changed from tapestries to lighter materials or wall paper.

The hallmark of British plain textiles, whether silk, wool, or worsted, was their quality. The basic materials were good, the dyestuffs consistent, the spinning even, the weaving regular, they were carefully packed and baled — and their price was always fairly high. Some markets were lost even in the Middle Ages for this reason, and there was a constant battle with the French for European and overseas markets, the latter envying what they regarded as

7. From book of worsted samples exported by John Kelly of Norwich, 1763. Intended for Spain/Portugal, but a bodice of the bottom swatch was found in Switzerland. *V & A — X.1745 (67–1885).*

superior British trading methods (though never conceding that British goods were anything but slightly inferior to those of France). As labour constituted a considerable and inevitable portion of the costs, the Combination Acts (forbidding the forming of trades unions) were early applied to the woollen and worsted industries. Labour costs also gave the underlying incentive for the technological advances of the 18th and 19th centuries. An examination of English and French pattern cards of the 18th century show no startling differences. If a truly English style can be detected, it is in the products of the silk industry.

From early in the 18th century we can follow the development of English silk design and compare it with that of France, owing to the survival of over a thousand dated English silk designs from 1706–56 and a collection of very important weavers' and other pattern books dating from the mid-18th to the mid-19th century. The design of silks changed with the season faster than the cut of the dresses or mens' waistcoats for which they were intended. The closer to Court they were, the more likely people were to change their fashions. Fashionable silks and their embroidered counterparts were elaborate and expensive but proportionately no more so than any modern symbol of wealth and prosperity.

From 1700 to about 1710 designs were constructed from a conglomeration of extraordinary motifs derived from exotic and European sources as well as purely imaginary shapes. These silks, known by the convenient term of "bizarre," often have a diagonal slant and are markedly elongated. The English versions which we see through the eyes of the young James Leman (1688–1745) were simpler with more recognisable motifs and a greater sense of balance in their composition (Fig. 10) than the wilder French designs. It was at this time that the English industry benefited

from French economic difficulties during the Wars of the Spanish Succession, and, thanks to British command of the sea, English silks began also to be exported. In the teens bizarre motifs retreated behind a mass of semi-naturalistic foliage (pages 69 top; 70 left); while silk design in the 1720s was dominated by the "lace pattern," in which a framework of diapered panels surrounded a formal bouquet of foliage arranged on a point repeat (Fig. 11). The most elaborate lace patterns date from c.1728–30 when hardly any clear ground was left on the silk . In the designs of Anna Maria Garthwaite (1690–1763) we can begin to see a subtle change about 1731–2 when floral motifs grew larger and began to dominate the "lace" (Fig. 12).

A violent reaction to the exploitation of surface texture took place in the thirties. Instead, Lyon designers initiated a quest for three-dimensional effects — in what is essentially a two-dimensional medium. The style was speedily adopted in England by Anna Maria Garthwaite, who indeed copied directly a design by Jean Revel, the most important figure in this movement. Designs grew larger in motif and in scale to give the most telling effects — the most striking perhaps are those of the year 1734, in which trees and disproportionately large flowers are arranged in space (page 69, bottom). Designs grew steadily larger until c.1740–42 (Fig. 13) when their repeats were usually about 28" long (the silks were 21" wide) and might even extend in damasks to 44", the full length of a sack-back dress. English silks of the thirties have crisp, clear colouring with a predilection for a golden khaki colour, crimson, a rich shade of emerald green, and gold and silver thread of high quality. Up till this point, although English silks can be easily distinguished from the French, the initial impetus in design came from France.

From about 1743 until 1765 Spitalfields produced a range of silks (of which the most typical was a brocaded design on a

10. Design for a satin tissue, dated 1708, by James Leman (c. 1688–1775), a designer and silk manufacturer. Property of Vanners Silks No. 46. *V & A — Q.509.*

white ground) which owe little, if anything, to France. Instead of purely conventional floral motifs there was a genuine attempt at botanical naturalism — a stylistic development which accorded with English interest in botany and gardening at the time. We can see both in Garthwaite's designs and many surviving silks (photo 14) flowers from the garden or hedgerow, daisies, holly, carnations, and roses scattered apparently casually across an open silk ground, sometimes a satin, but characteristically a lustring which allowed the intrinsic quality of the silk to be seen at its best. The flowers usually form an asymmetrical cartouche — for this is the period of the rococo — and towards the end of the 1740s such cartouches appear in self-coloured patterns in the background of the design (page 148, left). During the 1750s floral decoration gradually became once more conventional (page 9, top), and by the 1760s English design seems to have lost its impetus. Once more Lyon was followed as closely as possible (it needed only a few weeks to get a pattern from Lyon and a silk onto the market), although both quality and colouring remained excellent. Fashions were changing. Printed cottons were challenging the supremacy of silks, and from the 1770s the softer, more romantic silhouette of ladies' clothes had no need of the stiff and gaudily patterned silks at which Spitalfields excelled. England never produced furnishing silks on the scale of firms such as that of Camille Pernon in Lyon, and there was no English Philippe de Lasalle. The pattern books of the period do, however, reveal the imagination which it was possible to exercise in choice of colour and motif even when designs had to be small and limited in cost (Fig. 15).

Throughout the 18th century and indeed until the second quarter of the 19th century the silk industry was concentrated in London, with silk throwing carried on increasingly in other centres for the London industry. Especially important were

13. RIGHT. Children of Lord Fauconberg by Philippe Mercier, 1742. The child on the left wears a pink dress brocaded in silver thread. Property of Capt. V.M. Wombwell. *National Portrait Gallery — 1383.*

14. FAR RIGHT. English brocaded satin, Spitalfields, 1744. Woven by Captain John Baker, design by Anna Maria Garthwaite, T. 393–1971, p. 27. Property of Sherborne Museum. *V &A — GB 4159.*

Somerset and Dorset in the West Country and in the Midlands Derby, Macclesfield, Congleton, and Leek. Eventually, some of these centres began to weave certain classes of goods, notably Macclesfield, which produced cheap silk handkerchiefs by the end of the 18th century. Gauze weaving was taken to Glasgow, and in Manchester low-grade silks were woven in the late 18th and even more in the early 19th century. Fashionable materials — and many others — continued, however to be made near the centre of fashion, the Court, Parliament (always useful in times of economic crisis), and near the biggest and richest market of all, London itself. The expanding overseas and especially the American market gave the industry confidence, and its loss was a disaster. The silk industry's success depended upon a high degree of specialist skill displayed by outworkers on piece rates working for numerous small firms, specialists in damasks, plain tabbies, rich brocaded silks, mens' suitings, etc., sometimes preserving their working relationship for two or even three generations. The draw loom on which patterned silks had to be woven demanded skills unnecessary on the later jacquard. The industry was organised in branches according to the materials made, and between 1773 and 1826 piece rates were fixed between masters and men and were enforceable by the local magistrates. While the Spitalfields Acts gave half a century of industrial peace, the extension of the Combination Acts to the silk industry made the forming of trades unions a criminal offence, and there were some bloody incidents between 1763–1769 (linked to a number of general social and economic causes). French silks were also prohibited from 1766 to 1826, a measure secured by two years of agitation and lobbying. The silk industry flourished under a system of protection and regulation.

The basis of this industrial organisation was completely undermined by developments in the woollen and cotton industries. The Industrial Revolution was created by and partly responsible for an enormous expansion in demand both overseas and at home. There was a rise in the gross national

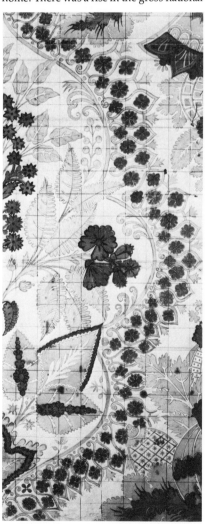

11. Design for woven silk to be brocaded with metal thread, almost certainly by Christopher Baudouin, 1723–4. *V &A — FD 950 (5973.17).*

product in the 18th century in England, and the textile industries benefitted. The textile inventions of the 18th and 19th centuries can be considered from many standpoints (economic, political, social, and technological) but only very indirectly from an aesthetic viewpoint. One principle holds good in general: the pattern of inventions works from later to earlier processes as each refinement speeds up the demand for more primary material. The flying shuttle patented by John Kay in 1733 created a demand for more thread than hand spinners could supply, hence Hargreaves' spinning jenny (1767) and Crompton's mule (1779). Carding and combing devices followed. Even when built of wood with the minimum of movable iron parts, machines of any kind were very expensive for hand weavers and their wives (any competent weaver or the local joiner could make a hand loom); it was thus more economic for the man with a little more capital than his fellows to concentrate, say, a number of jennies together and to work them all by water power. This led to a concentration of the textile industries (wool and cotton) along valleys with fast-moving streams such as the Colne Valley between Lancashire and Yorkshire and Airedale in Yorkshire's West Riding. There was no immediate overnight change, and hand and machine processes continued together in the same industries until the 1840s. Each textile industry generated its own inventions and refinements. The silk industry did not use the flying shuttle, for its fabrics were only 21–22 inches wide, but it did adopt the jacquard loom towards 1840 after an abortive introduction in the early 1820s. Silk is thrown from long filaments, and it was important to get a strong and even warp of the right quality. Hence Sir Thomas Lombe successfully copied Italian organzine mills and set up a factory (on the river Derwent in Derby) worked by water power in 1718. Apart from organzine the work of silk throwing could be successfully

15. FAR LEFT. From a book of weavers' samples, 1776. English (Spitalfields), possibly by the Bachelor, Ham, and Perigal firm. Warner Archive. *V & A — GD 4861 (T.374–1972, p. 127).*

16. LEFT. Man's coat of French silk, c. 1727–29. The lining of block-printed cotton is probably English from the same period. *V &A — R 1109 (1182–1899).*

carried out by hand, partly in factories and partly by outworkers. Women and very young children were employed, and their labour was cheaper than any machine.

Cotton

Cotton was imported from the Near East and used in fairly small quantities in the 17th century, and references to "cottons" are as often to coarse woollen cloths as to real cottons. The growth of cotton in the American colonies and its export to Great Britain created a new industry. Whereas the raw material for the silk industry had always to come from foreign countries and had to pay numerous high duties, the production of cotton was under British control. It was used with linen initially because the technical problems of making a cotton warp were not easily overcome. Such cloths were known as "fustian" in the 18th century. It was otherwise easier to process than linen, and it was quickly adopted for cheaper clothes and furnishings. Its arrival coincided with the fashionable demand for painted Indian cottons deplored by the silk and woollen interests in the late 17th and early 18th centuries. The advances in theoretical chemistry in the 17th century benefitted the European calico printers, who sought to imitate Indian products. Both in Holland and in England by the late 17th century printers had learnt how to print madder successfully in a whole range of shades. In the 18th century indigo, a much more difficult dyestuff, was mastered. Some colours were printed, others "pencilled," or painted by hand. On linen and cotton mixtures there was a speckled effect, since dyestuffs do not take as well on linen. At first designs tended to be in the Indian manner (Fig. 16), with a fairly restricted range of colours. By the middle of the 18th century the colour range had expanded, and designs were in keeping with European silks and embroideries (Fig. 17).

In 1752 the firm of Nixon at Drumcondra in Ireland produced a startling new invention, large-scale patterned furnishings printed in monochrome from copperplates. On practical grounds cottons had long been

12. Design for a woven silk by Anna Maria Garthwaite (1690–1763). *V &A — FD 951 (5975.8).*

able to compete with wool and silk. In the 1750s for the first time the calico printers were able to produce a fabric which could compete with silks in the most fashionable markets — and was itself a fabric with which neither silk nor wool could compete. The design of these early calico prints epitomises the best in 18th-century decorative art with a nicely balanced mixture of decorative and naturalistic elements tastefully arranged. Nixon soon transferred his factory to England, and a series of excellent factories followed his success: Collins at Woolmers (who incorporated the pagoda at Kew into one design), the Wares at Crayford (who produced some charming printed handkerchiefs), Robert Jones (page 159, right) of Old Ford (who was responsible for some of the most famous and beautiful designs), and the Bromley Hall factory founded by the Ollive, Talwin, and Foster families, some of whom had been calico printers as long ago as the late 17th century. Although the first calico printers were established near London, by the late 1730s the centre of the cotton industry had shifted to Lancashire. The Act which legalised the printing of linen and cotton mixtures (which had been going on since the printing of pure cottons had been forbidden in 1721) was known at the time — 1736 — as the "Manchester" Act. It remained in force until 1811. Printed cottons were produced for every market, from cheap servants' clothing to the immense quantities of excellent furnishings exported. They served all purposes — bed hangings and window curtains (even the conservative George II began to have chintzes in the 1730s), petticoats, dresses, handkerchiefs, and quilts. Special quilt centres were printed in the early 19th century for ladies to incorporate into their patchwork (page 198, left). Colours were good and, apart from yellow, mostly fast. Block-printed chintzes continued as well as copperplate — the Peels of Bury (relatives of the politician) produced excellent

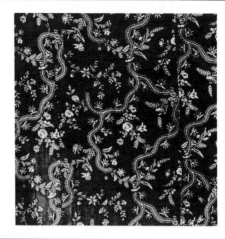

17. RIGHT. From the album of Barbara Johnson, kept from 1746–1823, with samples of fabrics for her clothes. This page has printed cottons, 1746–8, similar in style to the silks she was wearing. *V & A — GD 4862 (T.219–1973).*

18. FAR RIGHT. Detail from a dress of English block-printed fustian, c. 1780–90. *V & A — GB 2831 (T.216–1966).*

block-printed cottons, as did Bannister Hall for Richard Ovey of London and the Matley family of Hodge near Mottram in Cheshire. Fashions changed very rapidly in both colours and designs, but one feature which should be singled out is the use of a very dark ground in the late 18th century and early 19th century (Fig. 18), which is perhaps unexpected to those accustomed to think of pale "regency" colours — which are mostly derived from 19th-century copies of faded textiles. So splendid were the English copperplate-printed textiles that later generations wrongly attributed to France many English cottons before the research of the late Peter Floud revealed their true origins. Flat copperplates engraved and applied by hand were, however, extremely expensive and copperplate-printed cottons slow to produce. A method was therefore sought whereby such materials could be printed by some mechanical method. Roller printing may seem obvious, but it was not an easy solution. There were many technical problems to be overcome to make sure that the dyestuff was taken up evenly, the cloth kept at the same tension, etc., and as the first rollers were rather small, the patterns tended to be rather squashed and foreshortened (Fig. 19). Apart from the use of lithography in the 1830s and 40s and screen printing in the 20th century, woodblocks (often with brass wire to make the pattern), roller, and plate printing (the latter for handkerchiefs) remained the chief cotton-printing methods, despite many refinements. The most noticeable changes in the 19th century were a widening range of colours from mineral sources, culminating in the aniline dyes of 1856 onwards and including a valuable (but at first poisonous) solid green. Until then green had to be made from blue (indigo) overprinted with one of the yellows, and since these were much less fast, the green has disappeared. Accompanying this was an increasing eclecticism most noticeable in the 1840s.

Shawls and Ribbons

The softly draped outline of fashionable ladies' costume in the late 18th century needed plain, soft fabrics — muslin, cotton, and sarcenet (if silk were used at all) — and thus fashion accessories became very important, ribbons and shawls especially.

Ribbons

Ribbons had been woven in London and in Coventry since the 17th century, both on single hand looms and on engine looms on which several were woven at once. None have survived from the 17th century which we know are English, although their appearance must have been much like their continental equivalents (Fig. 20). Their importance in fashion fluctuated violently, and it was an industry subject to frequent booms and depressions. In the late 18th century ribbons became so important that Heideloff devoted the frontispiece of his Gallery of Fashion for 1794 entirely to woven ribbons. They trimmed hats as well

19. English cotton, roller-printed in blue with a roller only 10 inches in circumference, c. 1811–15. *V & A — GD 4869 (T.154–1958).*

as the edges of dresses and formed simple sashes with long, flowing ends trailing gracefully. The earliest known Coventry ribbons are in a weaver's pattern book dating from 1809–12, and they are in the severely Neo-Classical taste of the day. Coventry remained the centre of an important British ribbon industry until the 1860s (pages 204-205), despite competition from France after French silks and ribbons were allowed into the country on payment of duty for the first time since 1765. Firms who made picture ribbons survived better than those who tried to continue in the millinery trade, for these encapsulated examples of high Victorian art had an immediate popular appeal that they have never lost. The floral ribbon shown by Coventry in the 1851 exhibition was a measure of their skill (page 205, right).

Shawls

The most admired accessory to the plain dresses of the late 18th century was the expensive and exquisite Kashmir shawl. Naturally enough, home industries sought to compete, although they never succeeded in making a cloth as fine or as soft. Shawl weaving was encouraged by premiums in the late 18th century in Edinburgh, and the first shawls were attempted in Paisley in the early 19th century. In Spitalfields all silk shawls were made in the European, not the Indian style. They were indeed virtually the only large-scale patterned fabrics produced there at the time and are exceptionally graceful (page 72). Norwich was one of the leading centres of shawl weaving. The city had a long tradition of textiles. They had made worsteds, half silks (silk and worsted or other fibres), and even pure silks at the end of the 18th century, and thus the city had plenty of experience in the necessary fibres, in serving a fashionable market, and in selling their goods all over the world. In France too there were earnest attempts to compete with the Kashmir shawls. Al-

though the French were initially ahead technically, it is not very easy to distinguish French and British shawls. While Paris and Paisley competed in the market for the "Indian" type of shawl, Lyon and Spitalfields produced the same kind of silk shawl in the early 19th century, and subsequently Norwich and Lyon produced fairly similar products. It was necessary for them to do so, for fashion had become international. In the early 19th century long, fairly narrow shawls had a deep border of well-disciplined cones at each end containing well-defined flowers (page 194, top left). Borders grew deeper, cones larger, and colours wilder. The plain central area shrank, while the floral decoration within each cone gradually escaped till it waved about in sinuous profusion in the late 1840s and in to the early 1850s. Before shawls ceased to be articles of high fashion about 1870, the decoration had once more been confined but within a series of compartments and cartouches (page 195). The later shawls were very large in order to accommodate the large crinoline dresses of the period — as we can see from early photographs.

The demand for larger patterns in the later 1830s at last made it economic to apply the jacquard loom to shawl weaving. Thus the initial cost, and it was considerable, of a pattern needing several thousand cards was spread over hundreds if not thousands of shawls.

British Textiles from the Mid-19th Century

The power loom invented by Cartwright in 1784 made slow progress at first. There were immense technical problems in the machinery and the materials for the machinery, and there were a whole series of inventions by different people before the power loom became a practical economic proposition. Power looms with steam instead of water power altered the social and economic basis of the industries they

served. Large amounts of capital were needed to set up the factories, and a new class of engineers and technicians were needed to keep the looms at work. A machine-tool industry developed. On the other hand, the conditions of the factory hands in the early 19th century were continually depressed. There were no guild restrictions on their numbers, no Spitalfields Acts to protect their pay, no legal sanctions to protect their working conditions or hours of work. The Parliamentary reports from the late 18th to the mid-19th century make horrifying reading.

Textile industries proliferated. Heathcote's first invention of machinery to make bobbin net dates from 1808, and by the teens no hand-lace maker could compete with machine-made net except for the highest-quality work. The jacquard was applied to lace making about 1840, making it possible to produce patterned nets for costume and lace curtains of great scale and complexity. The processing of shoddy (the recycling of used cloth) and cheap Indian cotton brought new clothes within reach of the poor (but employed) worker. He could

22. Woolen-pile picture after Landseer's *Dignity and Impudence*, woven by John Crossley & Sons, Halifax, 1850–69. *V & A — GC 1356 (T. 60–1929).*

even have a patterned waistcoat after the technical problems of weaving a worsted with a cotton warp had been solved — for this was a much cheaper fabric. The invention of the sewing machine brought into being an important industry — ready-made clothing — eventually in standard sizes. Such clothing had existed before but to a very limited extent. The 18th-century gentleman could buy a set of waistcoat "shapes" for his tailor to make up — giving more or less fullness to the back as the customer's own shape required. Cloaks, stockings, and gloves had always been obtainable ready-made, but if the poor bought ready-made clothes they bought them second-hand. Naturally, high-quality woollens and worsteds continued to be made for the middle and upper classes. These would be individually tailored as they had always been. Beau Brummell set the fashion for plain, dark suits for men — a fashion which has lasted for over a hundred and fifty years. The demand for plain, high-quality facecloth in dark blue, black, or occasionally brown by this time provided the backbone of the Yorkshire woollen and worsted industries. There were variations with dark coats and light trousers with perhaps a check or herringbone pattern, but, once established, they have lasted with hardly any change until the third quarter of the 20th century. The only 20th-century innovations were to add a range of bluish greys to the normal range of middle-class, middle-aged mens' clothes, while nylon or terylene have been introduced in the last twenty-five years for added strength. If men grew increasingly sober in their dress, both their ladies and their homes were covered in often dazzling colours. Since the jacquard loom could make large patterns, it did so, and applied to the power loom it could produce thousands of yards of heavily patterned furnishings (Fig. 21). Equally, in coarse cotton a jacquard-woven tapestry 10' × 8' could be woven from, say, a picture by

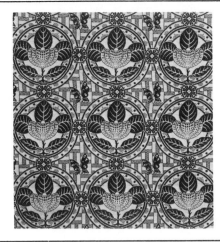

23. RIGHT. Cotton machinery of Messrs. Hibbert and Platt, illustrated in the 1851 Official Descriptive Catalogue of the Exhibition, Class 6, Vol. 1, facing p. 262. Catalogue in the V & A Library. *V & A — GD 4864.*

24. FAR RIGHT. *Butterfly Brocade*, designed by E.W. Godwin, c. 1874. Woven by Benjamin E. Warner's firm. *V & A — GD 4870 (T. 152–1972).*

Landseer, a popular choice of painting for the woollen pile pictures made by Crossley's of Halifax (Fig. 22). Artificial and synthetic colours had extended the range of the calico printer and the dyer, and it is clear both from photographs and from paintings that mid-Victorian families were not unduly worried by the presence of half a dozen strongly coloured patterns in one room. Very dark blues and browns, with bright green, orange, and red, seem to have been very popular. The style of the 1840s was predominantly naturalistic, but the overblown tea roses, a favourite motif, were often accompanied by decorative scrolls, a last whisper of the rococo. Roller printing of textiles with many fancy effects had advanced considerably, and some of the wildest flights of fancy occur in printed furnishing cottons.

Delight in the machine and its achievements was epitomised by the 1851 Exhibition. The machines themselves were on show, cast-iron monsters lovingly decorated with inlaid or raised patterns in brass and the wonder of the world (Fig. 23). Raw materials, hanks of wool, and also textiles were shown, and in the Catalogue we can see their illustrations and marvel at the number of jacquard cards or the number of colours, but hardly ever can we discover the name of the designer.

A reaction against completely eclectic design was evident as early as the 1830s. A Select Committee of the House of Commons, which examined the problems of Arts and Manufacturers in 1835, recommended the founding of art schools and museums. The latter should contain examples of good design in different fields, should be free, and art students should be encouraged to use them. There had been such a school and museum in Lyon since the 18th century, which was frequently cited by witnesses. Thus it was hoped to educate British designers and win overseas orders in the quality as well as the utilita-

rian markets. The first of the government Schools of Design opened its doors in June 1837, and several followed in different parts of the country, including schools in Spitalfields and Coventry. Another, possibly stronger influence came from Japanese art, which began to reach Europe in the middle of the 19th century. The restrained use of colour and the orderly and balanced use of pattern, with the essential nature of floral forms brought out but used entirely decoratively, had a marked influence on several important designers such as E. W. Godwin (Fig. 24) and Bruce Talbert, who designed some very successful textiles with a marked Japanese influence.

William Morris and the Arts and Crafts movement combated eclecticism from a totally different standpoint. They rejected the machine and its products and strove to produce beautiful objects without it, drawing their inspiration from the Middle Ages. Morris founded his own firm in 1861, and his textiles have remained influential to this day. He also took an interest in embroidery, although the greater part of the

25. Detail of panel designed by William Morris and Edward Burne-Jones for Rounton Grange in Northallerton. Embroidered by Margaret Bell and Florence Johnson between 1874–1882. *William Morris Gallery, Walthamstow.*

firm's work in this field was carried out by his daughter May and by G. F. Dearle. Morris himself often worked in conjunction with Sir Edward Burne-Jones, notably in a number of commissioned designs for the Royal School of Art Needlework and for private individuals. The embroideries for Rounton Grange are an important example (Fig. 25), worked by Margaret Bell and Florence Johnson. We see in this set his characteristic interest in a medieval subject (the Romance of the Rose), his skilful use of floral decoration, and his appreciation of the textural quality of embroidery. Linked with Morris in spirit if not commercially was the Leek Embroidery Society, dominated by the Wardles (the family of Morris's first dyer).

Morris's woven and printed textiles for furnishings were often on a very grand scale with long repeats to their patterns. The quality was excellent, as Morris intended it should be, and even early examples have worn well. He made detailed studies of textiles in the South Kensington Museum, yet his designs are not mere reproductions or pastiches. He paid enormous attention to the structure of both the design and the fabric itself. He even set up his own printing works at Merton Abbey because he was dissatisfied with the standards of commercial production. His designs are basically well-observed floral motifs treated decoratively — so that his "Honeysuckle" is essentially a plant, but its decorative possibilities are exploited. Occasionally he introduced some charming birds, as in "Peacock and Dragon" (Fig. 26) or "Strawberry Thief," and the same is true. He lectured on the necessity of decoration being suitable for its purpose and not excessive.

Benjamin Warner, a former pupil of the Spitalfields School of Design, had a rather different approach when he founded his firm in 1870. He was prepared to use mod-

26. FAR LEFT. *Peacock and Dragon*, designed by William Morris in 1878 and woven by Morris & Co. *V &A — M 74 (T.64–1953)*.

27. LEFT. Detail of hanging designed by Godfrey Blount, c. 1897. It is linen appliqué with some silk embroidery. This type of embroidery is found in the Liberty catalogues of the period c. 1900–1907, both on cushions and in hangings. *V & A — K.2487*.

ern dyestuffs and eventually even power looms to produce high-quality furnishings, but as far as he could he used first-rate designers in a modern technology. They included the architect Owen Jones (page 214), Bruce Talbert, E. W. Godwin, Sydney Mawson — a follower of Morris — Arthur Silver, and A. H.Mackmurdo of the Century Guild. The Warner ledgers from 1884–1930 show that only a few of the really well-designed textiles were popular in the market; the firm's trade rested on reproductions like that of many of its competitors. The Mortons in Carlisle and A. H. Lea of Birkenhead, equally important design studios of the day, had to produce much hack work as well as the designs for which they became celebrated. Nevertheless, British textile design became for a time extremely influential on the Continent. Liberty's, the shop in Regent Street, became the by-word for modern design. It was in Liberty's that the customer could buy furnishings in the style of *art nouveau*, whose influence in British textile design can be seen from the mid-90s. Designers like Lindsay Butterfield, Arthur Silver, and C.F.A. Voysey (pages 212, 215) produced exciting fabrics with the sinuous forms characteristic of the style, seen at their most extreme in the Paris Exhibition of 1900. The style pervaded dress silks, furnishings, and printed, woven, and embroidered textiles alike. A major innovation in embroidery at the end of the 19th century was the use of appliqué embroidery based on bold, clear shapes. These made their point not by the use of delicate stitches but by contrasting colours and textures. Leading but unrelated exponents were Godfrey Blount (Fig. 27), H. M. Baillie Scott, and some members of the Glasgow School of Art. Another important member of the Glasgow School, Ann McBeth, relied on a different kind of simplicity, teaching her pupils to create designs starting with the easiest stitches and insisting that elaboration of technique and design should move forward together.

The inspiration of the *art-nouveau* designers seems to have lasted until about 1905–6, and after that French, Viennese, and German designers took the lead. There was, alas, a regression by many manufacturers to the safety of repetitive "reproductions," often reproductions of 19th-century reproductions of faded 18th-century textiles. This was the taste of the most lucrative commissions: the opulent grand hotels and liners of the Edwardian era. An exception to this were the Omega workshops in whose brief existence from 1913–1919 such notable designers as Vanessa Bell, Roger Fry, and Duncan Grant produced design work of an *avant-garde* if not an entirely practical nature. Although an occasional British textile was praised at the Paris Exhibition of 1925, including an early rayon-and-cotton designed by Bertrand Whittaker for Warner's called "Marble" (Fig. 28), it was rather the quality of British worsteds than the design of British patterned fabrics which were commented upon. Taste pioneered in the Continent was eventually reflected in British commercial textiles. Possibly the

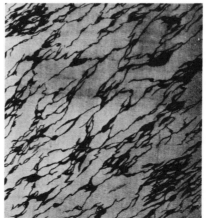

28. *Marble*, designed by Bertrand Whittaker, woven in cotton-rayon by Warner & Sons and shown at the Paris 1925 exhibition, where it was praised for its novelty. *V & A — GD 4871 (T.198–1972)*.

most enterprising firms of the 20s and 30s were William Foxton and Alan Walton, who employed some of the best designers of the time. A school of hand weavers came into being in this period, representing a new and opposing tendency, an interest in the texture of the materials themselves. Thus in the 1930s we find somewhat repetitive "Cubist" designs on everyday furnishings, but artist-designers like Ethel Mairet (Fig. 29), Enid Marx, and others turned weaving once more into an art in its own right. This development flowered after the Second World War in the work of such weavers as Peter Collingwood. It was paralleled in the embroidery carried out in many post-War art schools and fostered by the Needlework Development Scheme. A sewing machine with a swinging needle attachment was used as much as hand sewing, together with many unusual materials. Christine Risley has done much to encourage this virtually new art.

Scotland

Naturally, many textiles were produced in Scotland which belong to the general history of British textiles; they were as likely to be marketed in London as in Edinburgh and might be exported all over the world.

Serviceable hard-wearing, coarse cloth was produced locally in Scotland as in England and a few — but very important — archeological fragments survive. Tartans peculiar to each clan apparently became distinctive in the 17th century and were codified by the 18th century before they were suppressed after the 1745 rebellion. They revived slowly in the 19th century until Queen Victoria made tartans immensely popular by using them for the royal family. A fine and extremely tough worsted was used for "hard tartan," a cloth with a surface almost like fine sandpaper, quite unlike the modern woollen tartans. (Worsted, it must be remembered, is not only a different type of wool, but combing

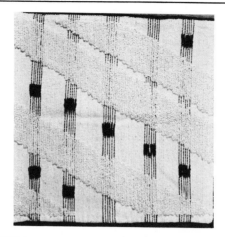

29. RIGHT. Cushion cover designed in 1935 by Ethel Mairet (1872–1952). *V & A — GD 4868 (T.154–1935).*

30. FAR RIGHT. Scottish Ayrshire work, c. 1825–30. Detail from a baby's gown. *Royal Scottish Museum — 1935.222.*

instead of carding makes its fibres lie very smoothly in the fabric.) The colours of tartans were derived from locally grown dyestuffs, remarkably constant in colour.

A linen industry was established in Scotland, and apart from coarse materials irrelevant here it produced three main classes by the early 18th century: a fine linen for printing, another for whitework embroidery, and a much heavier quality for table linen. Like the Irish linen industry, it was deliberately fostered in order to discourage either region from developing a woollen industry which could compete with the English. In the early 19th century the whitework embroidery was transformed by the introduction of needle-lace fillings which became famous as Ayrshire work (Fig. 30).

One of the local industries producing heavy materials began in the 19th century to earn a more than local reputation: namely, the heavy woollen twills intended for mens' clothing woven in the Hebrides on the island of Harris with Lewis. Protected and encouraged since the 1830s, despite many vicissitudes Harris tweed achieved and has held an international reputation. Another later 19th-century hand industry to earn a similar reputation was the Shetland shawl, as fine and delicate as the Harris tweed was rough and hardwearing (Fig. 31). Fair Isle knitting gave its name to a type of knitting pattern produced all over the British Isles but originally used in the Outer Hebrides for entirely practical garments.

By contrast, in what became one of the chief industrial areas of the British Isles, the Lowlands of Scotland, a number of modern industries were established: linen, cotton, silk, mixed goods, shawls, and carpets. Glasgow, Paisley, Galashiels, and Kilmarnock have been especially important to the textile industries.

Ireland

The importance of Ireland as a textile centre

dates from the 18th century when the Irish linen industry received government protection. Louis Crommelin was sponsored to set up a manufactory of linen damasks at Lisburn in 1698, a town where there was already a Huguenot colony. Irish linens found an immediate market in England and were also exported. Towards the middle of the 18th century a number of calico printers were established in and near Dublin (just as the linen weavers tended to be in or near Belfast), including Nixon, of whom we have already spoken. Irish calico printing continued to be distinguished until the end of the century. There was also a silk industry in Dublin, but unfortunately, no certainly authenticated piece of Irish-woven silk has come down to us. It can only be guessed that its products were similar to those of Spitalfields, but that it probably produced more plain than patterned silks — although it must not be forgotten that Georgian Dublin was a rich and fashionable market. Very important also was Irish production of half silks, that is, fabrics made of silk and wool or other

31. Detail of a Shetland shawl. Scottish, third quarter of the 19th Century. *V & A — GD 40008 (T.104–1961).*

fibres. Although poplin was made in London and elsewhere, it was Irish poplin that became so widely known.

Textile production continued undiminished in the 19th century, although its character changed. Linen damasks were eventually made on a jacquard, not a draw loom. Because of Ireland's poverty there were well-meaning attempts to set up other hand industries — notably lace — with moderate success. The 20th century has seen a decline in the importance of linen, but several other industries of greater importance appeared. In Donegal an important carpet-weaving factory was established in 1898, and it was also in Donegal that very fine high-quality worsteds for ladies' clothing have been woven. The good water, lack of pollution, and rich grass have produced an especially good breed of sheep, which grows a long, fine fleece. A number of successful manufacturers of fashionable materials have been established in Dublin since the Second World War, and their products are marketed around the world.

Carpets

When any floor covering was used at all for many centuries, it was in the form of a layer of rushes. By the 16th century these were generally woven into matting rather than scattered loose, and the designs for such mats have hardly changed since the 17th century. Rush matting came from Norfolk and still does, although in the 20th century it is also imported. Alternatives for the very rich, from the early 16th century on, might be an imported Turkish carpet, which, however, was much more likely to be used on a table than on the floor. Very occasionally from the late 16th century on a "turkey-work" foot carpet is mentioned in an inventory. Such carpets were the English or European copies of Turkish carpet techniques. Among the earliest and most splendid examples of turkey work are the

32. FAR LEFT. Detail of an English tur-
keywork carpet, dated 1585, woven in wool
on silk and copied from a Turkish carpet
belonging to the family. Property of the
Duke of Buccleuch. *V & A — 38376.*

34. LEFT. Illustration of carpet from the
Official Descriptive Catalogue of the 1851
Exhibition, class XIX 263. Patent velvet-pile
tapestry carpeting shown by Pardoe,
Hoomans, and Pardoe, Kidderminster. *V &
A Library — GE 73.*

carpets which belong to the Duke of
Buccleuch, in which the design as well as
the technique is taken from a Turkish carpet (Fig. 32). Even when the pattern was
thus derivative, the colours are those of
European textiles and the materials are
different. Turkey work was used for foot
and table carpets, for cushions and upholstery until the first half of the 18th
century. Embroidered carpets also imitating the patterns of contemporary Turkish
imported carpets were made from the late
16th century onwards, embroidered in
cross-stitch on a canvas ground.

Loom-woven carpeting of double or triple
cloth came into use in the 17th century.
Since it was less hard-wearing and just as
vulnerable to moths as turkey work, virtually none has survived. It can sometimes
be discerned in paintings and may have
been the ''Kidderminster stuff'' mentioned
in inventories. Inventories which were
usually made at the death of an owner for
his heirs are the chief source of information
on furnishings, but often their terminology
is obscure; it was not designed for readers
two or three hundred years in the future.
Thus the ''Irish ruggs'' which are often
mentioned are clearly a coarse blanket,
since they usually were found on beds and
not in the best rooms. Not until the 18th
century did weavers at Wilton adapt the
principle of velvet weaving to the making
of carpets. In 1741 Ignatious Couran and
others took out a patent for making carpeting of the kind known as ''moquette,''
which was normally imported from France.
This was later called ''Brussels'' carpeting.
The drawing accompanying the patent
shows a normal velvet loom, however. It
produced a regular, repeating pattern in
the style of the day. None has survived, but
in paintings it is possible to guess that it is
this which is covering the floor.
One design by the silk designer Anna
Maria Garthwaite was for a carpet, and the
small number of cords suggest that it was
for moquette of this type (Fig. 33).

Hand-woven carpets in the technique of
turkey work but in the grand style of the
French Savonnerie factory were also
attempted in the 18th century by Claude
Passavant, a serge manufacturer in Exeter
also by Thomas Moore, a hosier of
Moorfields who worked for Robert Adam,
and Peter Parisot, who had a factory at
Fulham in London. Good examples from
each factory have survived. The Axminster
factory set up in 1755 made hand-woven
carpets, sometimes copies of a popular type

33. Detail of carpet pattern designed by
Anna Maria Garthwaite, 1753. *V & A — FD
1264 (5989.30).*

of Turkish export carpet known as
''Smyrna,'' such as the one bought by Sir
John Soane in 1823.

Both the double-cloth and the looped
velvet-pile methods of weaving could easily be adapted to a jacquard, thus extending
greatly in the late 1830s and 1840s the range
of possible patterns. At the same time
various methods of imitating handmade
cut-pile carpeting were devised: the loops
of Brussels pile could be cut, chenille used
for the weft, and the warp of a Brussels pile
carpet printed before weaving so that the
pattern appeared when woven without the
use of a jacquard. Very soon totally new
structures were evolved which could only
be woven on machinery. These were and
are often highly complex, producing a
hard-wearing carpet with an immense
range of patterns. It is hard to summarise
the production of the last century, which
has included copies of famous eastern
carpets like the Ardabil in every possible
size and colour range, floral designs of
exceptional vulgarity (Fig. 34), *art-nouveau*
designs probably woven in Donegal,
avant-garde modern designs of the 1930s,
and even a few reasonably harmonious and
inoffensive patterns. Among the best of the
pre-1939–45 designers of carpets was Marion Dorn. The structure and quality of the
better-class products has been consistently
very good, as we can judge from many
carpets. It seems, however, to have been an
industry where the designer with an
aesthetic sense was far less in evidence
than elsewhere.

Natalie Rothstein
Deputy Keeper
Department of Textiles
Victoria & Albert Museum

*I would like to acknowledge the help of my
friends and colleagues Donald King, Valerie
Mendes, Wendy Hefford, Santina Levey, Avril
Hart, and Linda Parry in criticising and improving this all too brief account. — N.R.*

ENGLISH— 14-16TH CENTURY

TOP LEFT. Center detail on embroidered dressing cover, 1592. *V & A — 1375 (T262-1968).*

TOP RIGHT. Detail of Erpingham chasuble, embroidered in gold, 14th Century. *V & A — 590 (T256-1967).*

BOTTOM. Section of embroidered Bradford table carpet, late 16th Century. *V & A — 1187 (T134-1928).*

ENGLISH—17TH-CENTURY NEEDLEWORK, ETC.

LEFT TOP. Tent-stitch panel (motifs for applied work), early 17th Century. *V & A — 985 (T80-1954).*

LEFT BOTTOM. "Abraham and the Angels." Embroidered cover, mid-17th Century. *V & A — 1297 (443-1865).*

CENTER TOP. Man's cap, silk and metal embroidery, late 17th Century. *Fitzwilliam — 267 (T9-1947).*

CENTER MIDDLE. Tapestry-woven purse in wool, silk, and metal, 17th Century. *Fitzwilliam — T8-1961.*

CENTER BOTTOM. Judith and Holofernes in needlepoint sampler, 17th Century. *Fitzwilliam—T11-1938.*

TOP. Section of crewelwork curtain, dated 1680. *V & A—775 (1390-1904).*

BOTTOM LEFT. Section of sampler made by Jane Turner in 1668. *Burrell Collection—31/8.*

BOTTOM RIGHT. Embroidered casket made in 1656 by Hannah Smith, age 12. *Whitworth—MIM T14 (8130).*

ENGLISH—18TH-CENTURY WOVEN SILKS & EMBROIDERY—I

Silk weaving was a highly developed art in 18th-Century England, and its center was at Spitalfields (London).

ABOVE. Detail of embroidered Elizabethan bed valance with procession of goddesses. *Burrell Collection 29/184.*

TOP. Silk damask, brocaded with silk and dated about 1717. *V & A — 1579 (T148-1968)*.

RIGHT. Detail of an embroidery made in the mid-18th Century. *V & A — 1390Bii (T200 & A-1969)*.

BOTTOM. Woven silk made in Spitalfields about 1733-4. *V & A — 984 (T99-1912)*.

ENGLISH—18TH-CENTURY WORK—II

LEFT. Design (on paper) by Joseph Dandridge for a woven silk, 1718. *V & A—1486A (E4451-1909).*

TOP. Embroidery sampler by Sophia Ellis, 1785. *Fitzwilliam—T164-1928. Glaisher Bequest.*

BOTTOM. Embroidered chair seat. Wool and silk on linen, 1725-50. *V & A — 999 (T188-1930).*

RIGHT. Embroidered center of a pillowcase, 1720. *V & A — 1091 (T123-1964).*

THE ENGLISH SHAWL & RIBBON—19TH CENTURY

The fashion vogue for shawls and ribbons in 19th-Century England has left in its wake an interesting range of patterned textiles and good source material for contemporary designers. The best of 19th-Century textile designers were meticulous craftsmen, and their skill is shown to its best advantage in the sharply etched detail of their shawls and ribbons. The two examples shown here are quite representative.

LEFT. Border on a silk dress shawl woven during the early part of the 19th-Century. The center section of the shawl is unpatterned. *V & A — 1489A (T218-1957).*

RIGHT. This brocaded silk ribbon is something of a tour de force. It was made in Coventry, the center of Jacquard ribbon weaving, and it was produced to be shown at the Great Exhibition of 1851. It was therefore designed to show ribbon weaving at its most skillful. *V & A — 1869 (T29-1947).*

WILLIAM MORRIS & THE TEXTILE ARTS—19TH CENTURY

The arts and crafts of medieval times were a strong source of inspiration to William Morris. This shows up in all his textile-design work but especially in his tapestries.

ABOVE. The "Flora" tapestry was woven about 1885 at Merton Abbey. The figure is by Edward Burne-Jones; the rest by Morris. Wool on a linen warp. *Whitworth—MIM T6 (8353).*

TOP RIGHT. The "Wandle" chintz was designed by Morris in 1884. *V & A — 703 (T594-1919)*.

TOP LEFT. Roller-printed cotton of 1831, revealing the changes Morris later brought to textile print design. Among flowers are portraits of William IV and Queen Adelaide. *V & A — 996 (T68-1946)*.

BOTTOM. Threefold screen of embroidered silk by Morris, 1860-80. *V & A — 992. Lent by Geo. Howard.*

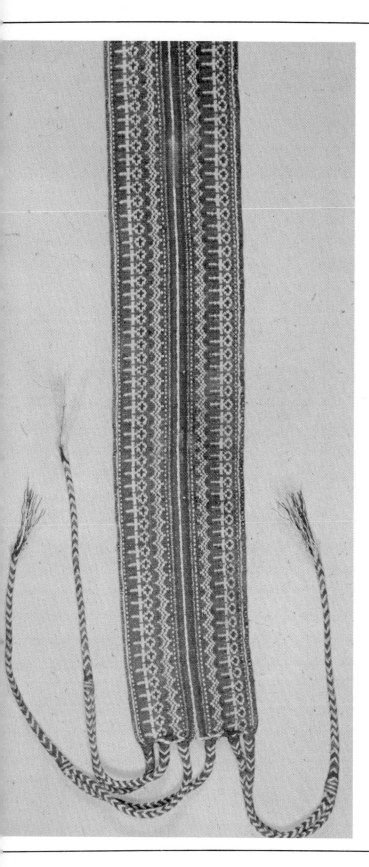
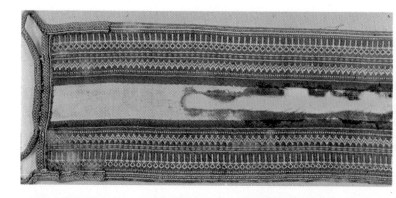
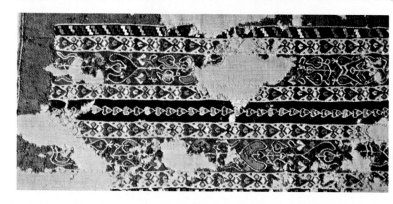

ANCIENT EGYPT—ANCIENT PERU

LEFT & TOP. The girdle of Rameses III, Egypt, 12th Century B.C. Tip end (left) is 1⅞ inches wide: the other end (top) is 5 inches wide, some deterioration. *Merseyside County Museums, Liverpool.*

MIDDLE. Coptic tapestry fragment from 6th-Century Egypt. *Whitworth—8426. Sir W. F. Petrie Collection.*

BOTTOM. Embroidered panel, Egypt, 5-6th Century. *Whitworth—MM252-1968. Manchester Museum loan.*

TOP. Peruvian woven textile from Paracas region, 500-200 B.C. *Museum of Mankind — K11833.*

LEFT. Graeco-Roman tapestry fragment from Egypt, 4th-Century. *Whitworth — 8426. Petrie Collection.*

RIGHT. Peruvian textile of the Chancay culture, 1000-1470 A.D. *Museum of Mankind — K17131.*

GERMAN & FLEMISH—14-16TH CENTURY

TOP. Rhenish tapestry altar frontal from Cologne, late 15th Century. "The Tree of Jesse" is the theme. Woven with wool, silk, gold, and silver yarns on linen warps. *Whitworth—MIMT3 (8247). Robinson Collection.*

LEFT. A late 14th-Century hanging from the Lower Saxony region of Germany. The work, applied on woolen cloth, is full of lively action reminiscent of the Bayeux Tapestry. *V & A — 1373 (1370-1864).*

ABOVE. The Three Fates in a charming millefleurs tapestry, Flemish, 16th Century. *V & A — 919 (65-1866).*

CARPETS AS TEXTILE ART—PERSIA, INDIA, CAUCASUS, TURKEY

TOP. Border detail of "Chelsea Carpet." Persia, 16th Century. Knotted wool pile. *V & A—491 (589-1890).*

BOTTOM. Carpet with Fremlin arms. India, early 17th Century. Wool pile. *V & A—580 (a) 1 (IMI-1936).*

TOP. Detail of a Turkish rug made in the late 18th Century. *V & A — 979 (392-1880).*

BOTTOM LEFT. Knotted wool carpet from Karabagh, Caucasus, mid-18th Century. *Fitzwilliam — T1-1934.*

BOTTOM RIGHT. Kurdish prayer carpet from Anatolia. Knotted wool pile, 78 x 55 inches. *Witworth — 15194.*

CHINESE TEXTILE ARTS—16-18TH CENTURY

The art fabrics of China may at first seem too elaborate and ornamental for modern tastes, but closer examination reveals an inner world of motif and detail that is quite adaptable to contemporary textiles.

ABOVE. Chinese silk tapestry (*k'o-ssu*) made as altar frontal about 1600. *V & A —2462 (FE37-1972).*

TOP LEFT. Embroidered Taoist priest's robe, Ching period, 18th Century. *V & A — 706 (1620-1901).*

TOP RIGHT. Chinese woven hanging in silk tapestry weave, 17-18th Century. *V & A — 331 (T80-1957).*

BOTTOM. Chinese woven-silk picture of a Taoist paradise. Mid-18th Century. *V & A — 1523(a)i (T167-1970).*

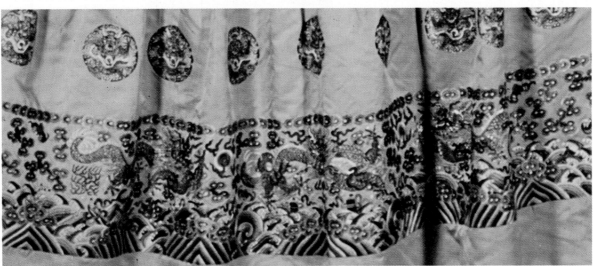

THE CHINESE ROBE AS ART—18-19TH CENTURY

Seen as art, the embroidered Chinese robes for court dress and religious ritual are masterpieces of skill. As wearable textiles, however, they are perhaps too exotic for today's cityscape (though often no more so than some dress and shirt prints). Yet here too, as in the k'o-ssu panels, there are many design motifs and colorings suitable for adaptation to modern textiles—especially to prints.

LEFT TOP. Embroidered Taoist ritual robe. Ching period, late 18th Century. *V & A—705 (T755-1950).*

LEFT BOTTOM. Chinese Emperor's court robe, embroidered, mid-19th Century. *V & A—2841A (T753-1950).*

ABOVE. Embroidered winter court robe, first rank. Chi'en Lung, 18th Century. *V & A—2843 (860-1896).*

INDIA—PAINTED-AND-DYED COTTONS

The cotton painters of India practiced a craft not unlike that of batik. It is technically known as mordant-and-resist dyeing. These skilled craftsmen were responsible for the great chintz vogue in Europe during the late 17th and early 18th Centuries. They produced their colorful cottons for export through the East India companies of Holland, England, and France. The word "chintz"

comes from the Indian *chitta*, which means "spotted cloth." The origins of these later chintzes can be seen in the borders of the hanging reproduced here. It was painted and dyed at Madras in the second quarter of the 17th Century and is a superb example of the craft. It is completely filled with intricate ornament and representational figures, yet all the diverse elements form a harmonious whole. And though the piece has an incredible amount of detail, it does not appear busy or overcrowded. The full panel is reproduced on the left. The other four photos are blowups of details.

V & A — 1467(a)i (687-1898).

INDIA—EMBROIDERY & PRINTS

The textiles reproduced on these pages were made about 1680, a time when export of Indian cottons to Europe was at its peak. In these fabrics we see the essential character of the decorated cottons that were so popular all over Europe and that fostered the competitive development of printwork in Holland, France, and England. The French block prints that copied the Indian cottons were known as "Indiennes."

LEFT. Not a print but an embroidery designed like one. Gujerat, c. 1680. *V & A —779 (IS154-1953)*.

TOP & BOTTOM. Details of two cotton hangings apparently produced by woodblock printing and dyeing rather than by hand painting. Shepherds and animals are the same in both fabrics. *V & A —776 (IS152-1953)*.

ABOVE. Blowup section of the fabric at left, showing block-printed figures in greater detail.

GREEK ISLAND NEEDLEWORK

TOP. Embroidered cushion cover from the island of Skyros. *V & A—2867 (T61-1950).*

LEFT. Embroidered cover, Epirus, 18th Century. 15 x 28 inches. *Whitworth—MIMT14 (8130). Lee Bequest.*

RIGHT. Embroidered skirt border from Crete. *Fitzwilliam—T39-1949. Daniel Gift.*

LEFT. Embroidered skirt border from Crete, made in the 18th Century. Like most embroideries from the Greek Islands, it is worked with silk yarns on linen cloth. *V & A — 1416A (2049-1876).*

RIGHT. Large bed-curtain or tent-door hanging from the Dodecanese island of Cos, embroidered about 1750. Its size is 92½ x 22 inches. *Whitworth — 14073. Mrs. P. B. Tillyard Gift.*

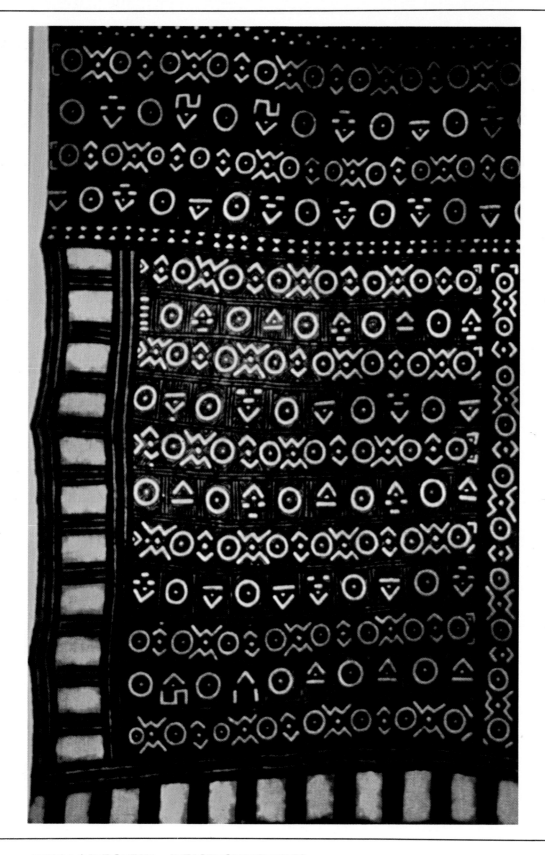

AFRICA & INDONESIA — INDIGENOUS TEXTILES

LEFT. Cassava-paste resist-dyed fabric *(adire eleko)* from Mali (Bambara). *Museum of Mankind — K6370.*

TOP. Batik from Central Java. Cotton skirt cloth, late 19th Century. *V & A — 1188 (IM265-1921).*

BOTTOM. Cotton batik, Java, 19-20th Century. *Museum of Mankind — K24386 (1934.3.7-70). Beving Bequest.*

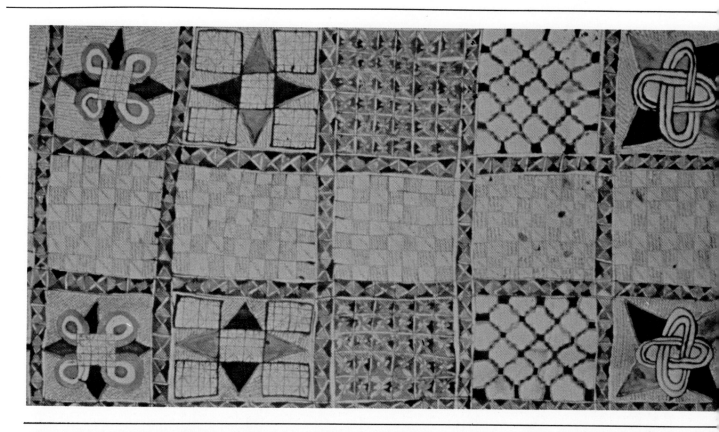

TOP. A stamp print on cotton from the Ashanti people of Ghana. This type of textile is known as *adinkra* and is made by printing with stamps carved from calabash gourds. *Museum of Mankind—K24380 (1951 Af3.1).*

BOTTOM. Examples of the textile stamps used by the Ashanti people in printing *adinkra* cottons. The stamps are carved from pieces of calabash gourds, to which handles are attached. *Museum of Mankind—K24389.*

AFRICAN TEXTILES—MODERN

Most general museums catalog their African textiles under the title "primitive"—an unfortunate choice since it carries derogatory overtones. A better choice might be "indigenous" or even "ethnographic." It is quite obvious that the textiles shown here are thoroughly sophisticated to modern eyes.

ABOVE. Woven textile from Togo (Kata) on the coast of West Africa. *Museum of Mankind—K1579.*

TOP LEFT. Stenciled resist-dyed cotton, Nigeria (Illa tribe). *Museum of Mankind—K24679 (1953 Af 17.18).*

TOP RIGHT. Stenciled resist-dyed cotton, Senegal (Ife tribe). *Museum of Mankind—K24384 (1953 Af 17.24).*

BOTTOM. A fine example of narrow-strip weaving from Senegal. It is 46 inches wide and consists of six separately woven strips that have been sewn together. *Museum of Mankind—K27775 (1934.3.7.195).*

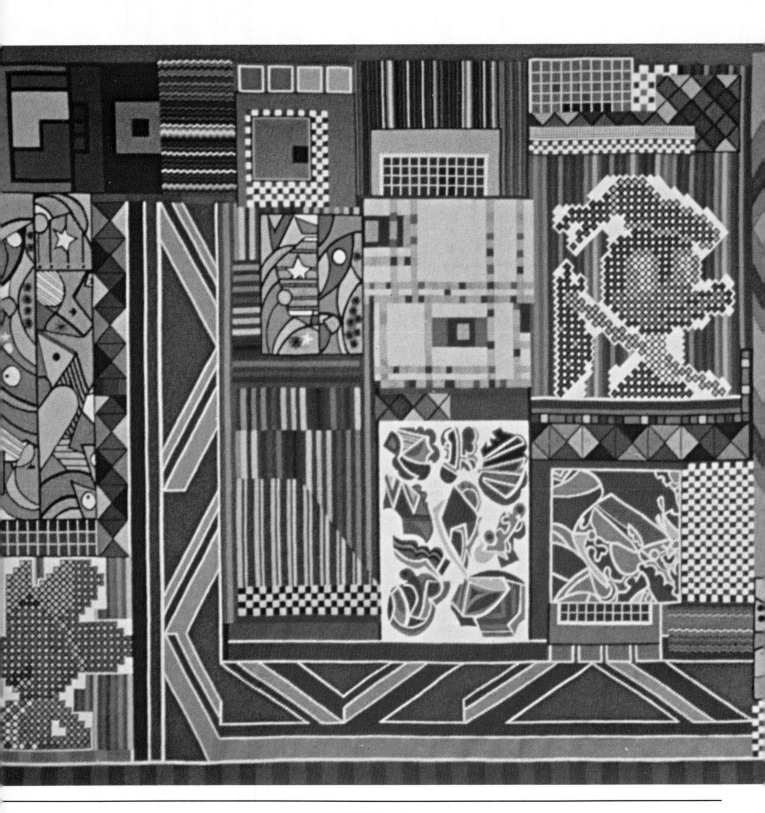

CONTEMPORARY ENGLISH TAPESTRY IN MANCHESTER

One half of the contemporary Whitworth Tapestry is shown here. It was designed by Eduardo Paolozzi as a commission from the Whitworth Gallery in Manchester to mark the opening of its new exhibition halls in March, 1968. The full size of the piece is 7 x 14 feet. It was woven of wool and polyester on linen warps by the Edinburgh Tapestry Company. It hangs in the Whitworth's main gallery. *Whitworth—MIM T9 (12315).*

TEXTILE DESIGN IDEAS

Beginning overleaf are 140 pages of B/W photographs showing a sampling of textiles held by museums in the United Kingdom and Ireland. It is a personal sampling. It reveals only the tip of the iceberg, but I believe it reflects the range and variety of textile-design ideas preserved in these collections. *** The pieces shown were chosen primarily for pattern interest — and only secondarily for historical importance. They are arranged in chronological sequence, but they cannot be seen as a photographic survey of textile-design history in all periods and cultures. That is not their purpose. *** Their aim is to suggest design themes for the fabrics of today through a photographic presentation of historic textiles preserved in the collections under review. At the same time these reproductions do reflect many high points in the global development of textile design. *** I hope the pictures will lead designers to the collections themselves — the most direct and consistently rewarding sources of design inspiration.

ANCIENT PERU — I. The graphic designs of ancient Peru are among the most fascinating sources for modern textile patterning. Perhaps this is because the abstract quality of the motifs appeals to modern eyes and because the symbolism is strange and unfamiliar to our western tradition. Fortunately, these qualities can be seen in actual textiles — both woven and embroidered — which date from at least 500 B.C. to the 16th Century and which have been eagerly collected by the world's leading museums.

FACING PAGE, TOP. Weaving from the Paracas region, dated 500–200 B.C. *Museum of Mankind — XI-34.*

FACING PAGE, BOTTOM. Embroidered border, late Paracas, 100–600 A.D. *Royal Scottish — 1933.397.*

BELOW. An "apron," tapestry-woven of cotton and wool. Nazca period, 100–700 A.D. *Royal Scottish — 1902.518.*

BOTTOM LEFT. Another example of late Paracas weaving, dated before 200 B.C. *Museum of Mankind — 30456.*

BOTTOM RIGHT. Also from the Paracas area, dating before 200 B.C. *Museum of Mankind — XI-35.*

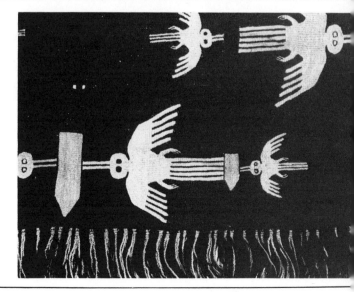

ANCIENT PERU — II. The U.K. and Ireland have at least eight collections of ancient Peruvian textiles, none very extensive but all typical of the culture in different periods. The two largest and most representative collections are those of the Museum of Mankind (British Museum Ethnography Dept.) in London and the Royal Scottish Museum in Edinburgh. More modest collections are owned by the V & A and the University Museum in Cambridge (under 100 pieces each). There are smaller but interesting groups of Peruvian textiles at the Bolton and Dublin museums; also at the Burrell in Glasgow and the Whitworth in Manchester.

FACING PAGE, TOP LEFT. Peruvian slit tapestry weave of the 14–15th Century. *Burrell — Inv. 225.*

FACING, TOP RIGHT. Chimu weaving from Pachacamac, dated 1000–1450 A.D. *Museum of Mankind — LXXXV-31.*

FACING, BOTTOM LEFT. Slit tapestry border of the 14–15th Century from Supe. *Burrell — Inv. 218.*

FACING, BOTTOM RIGHT. Detail of child's woven wool poncho, 14–16th Century. *Royal Scottish — 1895.423.*

ABOVE. Tapestry-woven wool apron of the 14–15th Century. *Royal Scottish — 1903.26.*

COPTIC TEXTILES — I. The term "Coptic" is considered something of a catch-all today because it covers so long a time span. However, it does serve to describe the characteristic wool-on-linen tapestry weaves which were made by the ancient Copts in Egypt from at least the 3rd to the 10th or 11th Century A.D. The Copts were a Christian minority in Egypt. (*Copt* is the Greek word for "Egyptian.") They did not practice mummification but buried their dead fully clothed. Because of this, many examples of their tapestry-decorated garments have been preserved in the dry soil of Egypt and thousands of these pieces — many only fragments — have been collected by museums all

over the world. The most characteristic form of traditional Coptic weaving is the roundel shown on the left. It is reproduced here about twice actual size.

FACING PAGE. Wool tapestry weave on linen ground, 6–8 Century A.D. *V & A — GA 3977 (T794-1919).*

BELOW. Egyptian wool tapestry, 4–5 Century A.D. *Ashmolean — 1941.1133. Newberry Collection.*

BOTTOM, Tapestry panel, wool on linen, 20 x 16½ inches. Egypt, 4th Century. *Whitworth — W.344 (8393).*

COPTIC TEXTILES — II. The collections of Coptic textiles in U.K. and Irish museums are rich and varied. At least 11 museums have holdings worthy of note. The largest and most representative is owned by the V & A, with over 2,000 pieces. Next in size stands the Ashmolean, with 800 pieces in its Newberry Collection. The Whitworth has some 600 pieces, including the famous group assembled by Sir William Flinders Petrie. At Bolton the Coptic pieces number a surprising 540, and at Merseyside there are over 375 examples, equally unexpected. Among smaller groups are those at the Royal Scottish (150), the Fitzwilliam (100), and the National in Dublin (61). Finally there are

token holdings — not uninteresting — in the British Museum, the Burrell Collection, and the Laing Art Gallery in Newcastle-Upon-Tyne.

FACING PAGE. Tapestry detail from Akhmin, 4–5 Century. *V & A — 52611 (243-1887).* THIS PAGE, TOP LEFT. Detail, 5th Century. *Burrell — Inv. 129.* TOP RIGHT. Wool on linen, 5–7th Century. *Merseyside — N61-730 (56.21.1000).* BOTTOM LEFT. Fragment, 4–5th Century. *V & A — 817-1903.* BOTTOM RIGHT. 6th Century. *Burrell — 137.*

COPTIC TEXTILES — III. Many of the Coptic tapestry fragments held by museums were woven as bands of wool decoration (claves) on shirtlike linen garments. (As such, they suggest the engineered prints of contemporary dress and blouse fabrics.) The weaving skill was of a very high order, with much carefully articulated detail compressed into small spaces and often with a lively sense of movement which we associate with Greek vase painting. The Coptic weavers were professionals catering to a market, and their style changed to match the tastes of Egypt's successive rulers. Thus, after the Arabs conquered Egypt in 641 A.D., Coptic designs took on a more abstract Islamic

character. Designs from this later period are shown on these pages.

FACING PAGE. A man's woolen tunic of the 8–9th Century in a rare state of preservation. It is four feet long. On the left is an enlarged detail. *Whitworth — W.327 (8358). Sir W. Flinders Petrie Collection.*

ABOVE LEFT. Coptic sleeve decoration, 7th Century. *Whitworth — W.326 (8362). Petrie Collection.*

ABOVE RIGHT. Coptic wool tapestry band, 26 x 4 inches. 7–8th Century. *Royal Scottish — 1911.269.*

284-1891

COPTIC TEXTILES — IV. The tapestry decorations on Coptic garments were woven at the same time as the garments themselves. The basic technique used is illustrated in the demonstration panel on the right. However, these decorations were highly prized and were often cut out of old garments to be appliquéd onto new ones. This is the way many of them were found when first uncovered from the shallow graves of Upper Egypt towards the end of the 19th Century. Woolen yarns were generally used for the tapestry work, and they were dyed in a subtle range of colors by blending a few basic vegetable dyes such as madder (red), indigo (blue), and Persian berries (yellow).

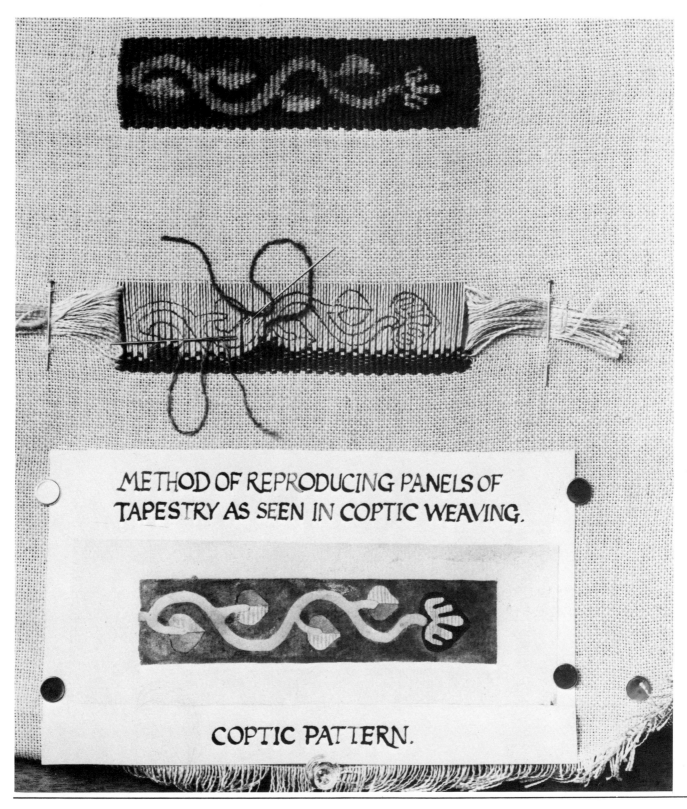

METHOD OF REPRODUCING PANELS OF TAPESTRY AS SEEN IN COPTIC WEAVING.

COPTIC PATTERN.

Further details on dyes, as well as yarns and constructions, can be found in Margaret Seagroatt's excellent booklet on "Coptic Weaves", City of Liverpool Museums, 1965.

LEFT. Detail of Coptic tapestry panel, 4–5th Century. *V & A — J1352 (284-1891).*

RIGHT. Panel by Mrs. Rolleston, presented by Lady Phillips to the Johannesburg Museum. *V & A — 48996.*

OPUS ANGLICANUM. "English Work" was the name given to the skilled ecclesiastical embroidery which gained fame throughout Europe by the middle of the 13th Century. It was greatly prized by both monarch and prelate for its workmanship and its splendor. Much of it glittered with silver and gilt, with seed pearls and semiprecious stones. The work was done in special London workshops by professionals who served a rigorous seven-year apprenticeship at the craft. The pieces shown here are among the finest remaining examples of an art form whose designers may also have been manuscript illuminators of the period.

CENTER & TOP. The Syon Cope. Late 13th Century. English hand embroidery. Silk and gold threads on a linen ground covered with red and green silk. Size is 115 x 56 inches. It depicts figures of the Savior, Virgin, Apostles, and six-winged cherubim. The structure of linked frames is typical of the period. Enlarged details of the border design are shown above the cope. *V & A — 66841 (83-1864)*.

LEFT. English embroidered stole with heraldic arms. Early 14th Century. *V & A — K 2080 (T40-1950)*.

RIGHT. English embroidered maniple, 1290–1340. Silk on linen ground. *V & A — K 2078 (T40a-1950)*.

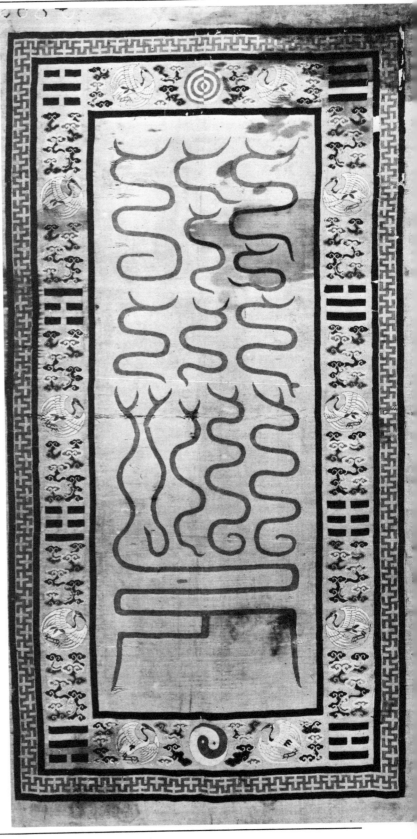

13–14TH CENTURY SILKS. There are obvious gaps in this picture sequence between textiles of ancient Peru or Egypt and silk art fabrics of the 13–14th Centuries. Missing are the elaborate silks of ancient China, some woven as early as 1600 B.C. Also absent are Byzantine silks from Constantinople (4th Century A.D.) and Sassanian silks from Persia (6–7th Centuries), as well as those from Baghdad (8th Century), Sicily (9th Century), and Spain (10–13th Centuries). Examples of textiles from these early periods do exist in U.K. museums, but their interest is more historical than graphic. They reproduce poorly as design ideas and have therefore been omitted. Such fabrics must

be examined at first hand. It is only when we reach the 14th Century that we find reproducible woven silk designs in the museums under review. A few are shown here.

FACING PAGE, LEFT. Sicily or N. Italy, 14th Century. Woven silk and gilt. *V & A — L582 (7087-1860)*.

FACING, RIGHT. Chinese woven silk, 14th Century. Taoist symbol of protection. *V & A — G865 (T164-1948)*.

TOP. Hispano-Moresque woven silk. Spain. 14th Century. *V & A — 67442 (1105-1900)*.

BOTTOM. Chinese woven silk panel. 13th Century (?). *V & A — M2134 (T746-1950)*.

TAPESTRIES, 15TH CENTURY. The medieval tapestry — which we may admire as art — is not usually a rewarding source of textile design ideas. The scale is too large and the themes generally too pictorial for adaptation. An obvious exception to this is the millefleurs tapestry, whose dense background of flora and fauna is excellent source material for print designers. Another exception might be the illustrative quality of many tapestries which suggests themes and design approaches for story-telling prints today. And there is an overriding aspect to any good tapestry which should interest students and designers. This relates to its function as a wall covering. It is

unobtrusive in the room, yet interesting. The colors, the figures, the composition of the whole complicated design are so well balanced that no one element obtrudes. Everything in the design is geared to achieve an overall texture which blends with the room.

LEFT TOP. Late 15th Century millefleurs fragment. *Burrell — 46/97.* LEFT BOTTOM. St. Pancras and St. Gothard. S. Germany c. 1460. *Burrell — 46/2.* ABOVE. Franco-Burgundian, mid-15th Century. *Burrell — 46/56.*

CHINESE SILKS & THE SILK ROUTE. The secrets of sericulture were discovered in China about 2640 B.C. They were jealously guarded and remained unknown in the West until about 550 A.D., but treasured silks from China were exported to the West from 100 B.C. or earlier. As highly prized as gold and rare jewels, they were carried westwards by caravan along the ancient Silk Route. It began at Sian and Lanchow and crossed the Great Wall and the desert of Takla Mahan to Kotar and Kashgar. It climbed the Pamir Mountains to Samarkand, then continued to Hamadan in Iran, to Baghdad in Iraq, and across the valleys of the Tigris and Euphrates to Palmyra in Syria. Thence

down to the Mediterranean at Tyre (Sur) and northwards to Antioch in Turkey. It was a treacherous route of some 6,000 miles, and it took almost a year to cover. The two woven silks (k'o-ssu) shown here are more recent but stem from that ancient tradition.

LEFT. Woven silk, China, 15th Century. One of a pair. *V & A — L 2059 (T101-1948). Vuilleumier Col.*

RIGHT. Woven silk panel, China, 1280–1368, Yuan period. *V & A — J1711 (T237-1910).*

WOVEN SILKS — SPAIN & ITALY. From the 10th Century on Spain was an important resource for luxurious woven silks. Weaving centers were located at Almeria, Malaga, Murcia, Seville, Granada and Saragossa. Spanish patterning was dominated by geometric figures and arabesques, often by the "laceria" design which resembles interlaced canework. Such designs we call Hispano-Moresque.

Italy became a great weaving center by the 14th Century, with flourishing industries in Lucca, Venice, Florence, Pisa, Genoa, and Perugia. Designs tended to be less regimented than previously, and constructions

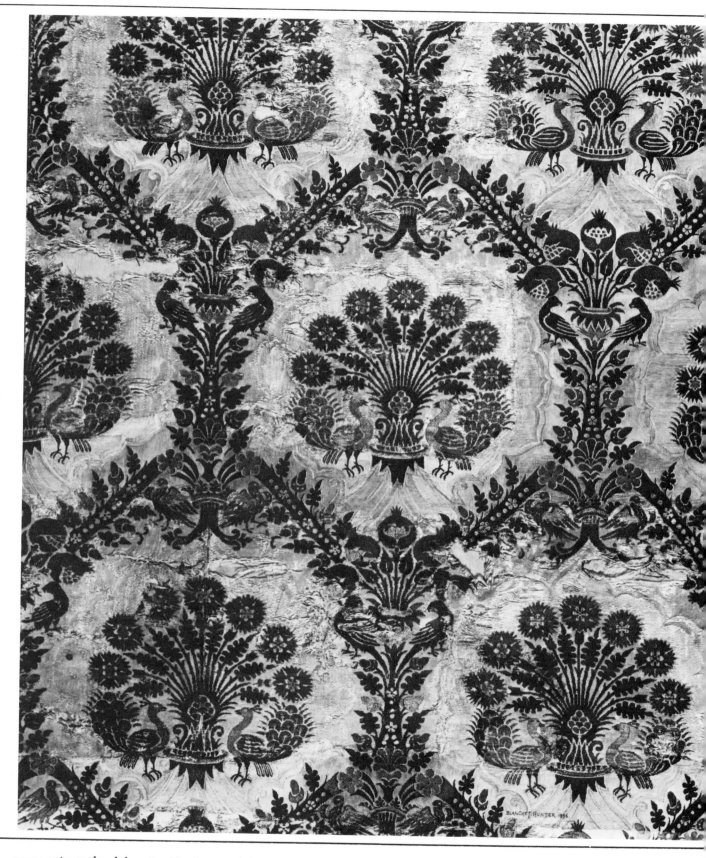

were extremely elaborate. Venice specialized in velvets, and in 1423 the city employed 16,000 skilled velvet weavers, divided into two crafts — one for solid colors, the other for patterns and brocades. Investment in the industry was 10 million ducats.

ABOVE. Brocaded silk damask, late 15th Century. Italy or Spain. *V & A — GB2027 (7611a-1861).*
LEFT. Woven silk with laceria design. Spain, 15th Century. *V & A — 67752 (1312-1864).*

TEXTILES OF PERSIA. It was the Persians who first acquired the secrets of Chinese sericulture (6th Century), and it was in Persia that silk weaving reached a high point of perfection under the Sassanian rulers in the 6th and 7th Centuries. A characteristic design was the medallion, often used as a frame for fantastic and stylized beasts or birds. But after the Arab conquest (641 A.D.) this ancient textile tradition faded and was not revived until the Safavid Dynasty (1499–1736). Textiles then became perhaps the most important manufactured products of Persia. In 1667 the city of Isfahan had some 32 weaving workshops attached to the court, each employing 150 skilled weavers.

Designs were made by the same court painters who produced the great Persian miniatures. From this period emerged some of the world's most elaborate fabrics — brocaded velvets on grounds of silver and gold. From this same textile tradition come some of the world's most renowned carpets — one of which is reproduced here. It is the famous Ardabil Carpet from the mosque of Sheikh Safi at Ardabil, woven in 1540. It is 34½ x 16½ feet and has about 30 million knots. LEFT. One half the carpet. RIGHT. Center medallion. *V & A — 67636 (272-1893)*.

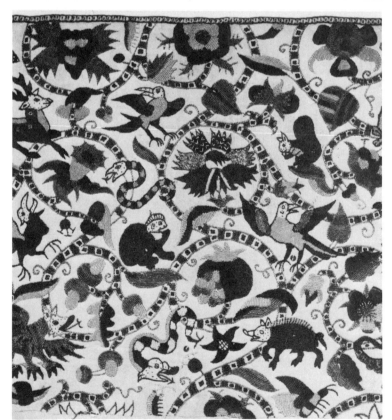

16TH-CENTURY MISCELLANY. LEFT. Vertical section of a typical decorated linen towel woven in Perugia during the 16th (or 15th) Century. Colors are blue and white. *V & A — 58126 (T12-1916).*

ABOVE. English embroidery of the early 16th Century. Black velvet and gold threads. *Burrell — 29/180.*

BELOW. Embroidered Elizabethan coif with coiling stem pattern. Late 16th Century. *Burrell — 29/22.*

TOP. Embroidered Scottish bed valance depicting the Adam & Eve story. *Burrell — 29/181.*

MIDDLE. Italian needle-lace border, about 1590. Width is 23 inches. *Royal Scottish — 1878.45.*

BOTTOM. Section of a long embroidered Elizabethan bed valance of the late 16th Century. The charming processional shows Flora and other Greek goddesses in a millefleurs setting. *Burrell — 29/184.*

17TH-CENTURY SILKS

LEFT. Woven silk from Italy or France, second half of 17th Century. *V & A — S1851 (143-1880)*.

ABOVE. Woven silk from Italy, late 17th Century. *V & A — Y549 (1225-1877)*.

BELOW. Italian brocaded damask, late 17th Century. *V & A — H735 (536-1896)*.

17TH-CENTURY VELVETS

ABOVE. Italian velvet, mid-17th Century. Detail is four feet square. *V & A — 52371 (4069-1856)*.

BELOW. Turkish silk velvet with silver thread, 17th Century. *V & A — 21679 (W.J. Myers Collection)*.

RIGHT. Italian velvet from Genoa, second half of 17th Century. *V & A — X2118 (118-1880)*.

INDIA, 17TH CENTURY — PAINTED & PRINTED. In India cotton was being spun as early as the 3rd millenium B.C., but the brilliant textile tradition we now associate with India did not flower until the Mughal Empire (1504–1707). The Mongol rulers who conquered India imposed a strong Persian influence on its arts and also fostered a great upsurge of textile production. The painted and printed fabrics shown on these pages come from this period and are prototypes of the chintz fabrics which created such a vogue in Europe. BELOW. Section of painted coverlet, Golconda, 17th Century. *V & A — FJ2533 (IS34-1969).*

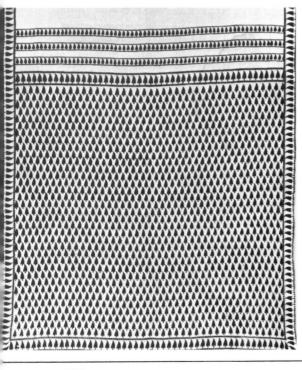

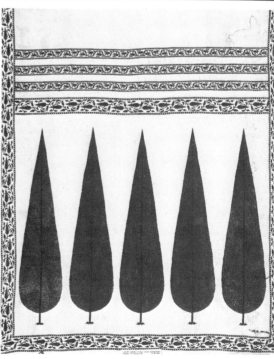

THE SAMPLER — 17TH CENTURY. The sampler flourished in England and other European countries during the 17th Century. Though many of them were made by children, they were often tours de force of technical skill in both embroidery and lace. They are rich in design motifs. Most museums in the U.K. and Ireland hold samplers, often of local origin. The largest and most diversified groups are those at the V & A, the Fitzwilliam, the Royal Scottish, and Ulster Folk museums.

LEFT TO RIGHT. (1) Italian needle-lace sampler, 17th Century. Detail. *V & A — Q399 (T 787-1919)*. (2) South German, 1688. Detail. *V & A — Q402 (104-1880)*. (3) English, 1660. Detail. *V & A — GX4815 (T217-1970)*. (4) English, 17th Century. Detail. *V & A — M1508 (829-1902)*. (5) Embroidery sampler, possibly Italian, 1649. *Nottingham — '07.78*. (6) Spanish embroidery sampler, 17–18th Century. Detail. Full size of sampler is 40 by 22 inches. *V & A — 39084 (241-1891)*.

PERSIA — 17TH CENTURY. During the Safavid Dynasty in the 16th and 17th Centuries, Persia (now Iran) produced some of the world's most consummate miniature painting under royal patronage. It also produced some of the world's most sumptuous textiles for export to world markets. A few are shown here.

BELOW. Detail of the renowned "Wagner" carpet, a classic example of "Persian Garden" design showing a fish-filled pond linking twin watercourses. 16–17th Century. *Burrell — 912*.

OPPOSITE, BOTTOM. Caucasian "Dragon" carpet, 17th Century, with stylized dragons. *Burrell — 9/38.*

LEFT TOP. Persian cut and voided satin velvet. Samarkand, 17th Century. *V & A — GB1323 (320c-1898).*

LEFT BOTTOM. Persian brocaded silk, 17th Century. *V & A — 74611 (555–1903).*

RIGHT. Silk embroidered Persian mat, 17th Century. 50 x 32 feet. *V & A — 47534 (172-1906).*

ENGLISH EMBROIDERY — 17TH CENTURY. BELOW. English needlework picture, embroidered in silk and metal threads, 17th Century. Such panels were by then frankly made as wall hangings. *Burrell — 29/122.*

BOTTOM. Detail of a famous embroidered English altar hanging, dated 1633. The ground is velvet. The embroidery is done in silver and silver-gilt thread. Silk cord and spangles are also used in raised and couched work. It may be the work of Edmund Harrison, royal embroiderer. *V & A — Z1212 (T108–1963).*

BELOW LEFT. English embroidered curtain, late 17th Century. Wool yarns on a mixed cotton/linen twill — an embroidery material first introduced in the 1630s. *Royal Scottish — 1934.548. Warren Bequest.*

BELOW RIGHT. English embroidered cushion cover of the 17th Century. *Burrell Collection — 29/192.*

BOTTOM. English crewelwork bedspread of the late 17th Century. Cotton twill ground. The "Tree of Life" pattern, with stylized earth base, is a frequent theme of painted Indian palampores. *Burrell — 29/188.*

17TH-CENTURY MISCELLANY

LEFT. Blue resist-dyed linen. Germany, 17th Century. *V & A — 53241 (774–1892). Forrer Collection.*

ABOVE. Knitted jacket with engineered patterning. Italy, 17th Century. *V & A — Z2251 (473–1893).*

BELOW. Section of embroidered miter. Italy, late 17th Century. Gilt on satin. *Royal Scottish — 1893–546.*

17TH-CENTURY NEEDLEWORK

TOP. Embroidered cover, silk on linen. Spain, 17th Century. *V & A — N1542 (1462–1892)*

BOTTOM LEFT. Embroidered coverlet, Persia, 17th or 18th Century. *V & A — Y126 (91–1897).*

BOTTOM RIGHT. Vestment, satin appliqué on velvet. Spain, 17th Century. *Royal Scottish — 1892.585.1.2.*

ENGLAND — 17TH-CENTURY NEEDLEWORK PATTERNS. Domestic embroidery was a flourishing movement in England from at least the early years of the 16th Century, and the need for design motifs was great. It was supplied by a proliferating series of pattern books, which were extremely popular and which ran into many editions. Such pattern books are excellent sources of small design motifs. The motifs are sharply detailed and are adaptable to all types of textiles — from prints to jacquard knits.

These pattern books can usually be found in the print departments of museums or in libraries. The Print Department at the V & A, for example, owns a large collection of pattern books from many European countries and from many periods. The designs reproduced here are taken from a 17th-Century "Sibmacher" pattern book belonging to the Samuel Pepys collection of prints at Magdalene College Library, Cambridge. They were made from a photostatic record of the patterns owned by the Fitzwilliam Museum's Textile Department.

CHINESE TAPESTRY — 17TH–18TH CENTURY. Our Western concept of tapestry weaving comes to us from European tapestries of the Middle Ages. We think of heavy structures with pictorial designs made in relatively thick wool yarns. The Chinese concept of tapestry weaving (k'o-ssu) is quite another thing. It is a very ancient art — fostered in China since at least the Sung Dynasty (960–1127) — and it uses very fine silk yarns rather than wool. This means that it can be extremely fine and intricate in detail as well as light in weight. Such weaving was used both for art hangings and for court robes.

Fine examples of the art come from the 17th and 18th Centuries. A few are shown here. They deserve close examination, because the overall designs may be too complicated for modern tastes but individual motifs can often provide rich source material. TOP. K'o-ssu panel, 17–18th Century. *Fitzwilliam — K2612 (T2–1972)*. BOTTOM. K'o-ssu, 18th Century. *Fitzwilliam — K2487 (T3-1972)*. RIGHT. One of eight k'o-ssu panels. Early 17th Century. *V & A — GB1371 (T269–G1971)*. FAR RIGHT. An 18th-Century altar hanging in silk tapestry weave is filled with design motifs, especially for print design. *V & A — 54569 (872–1901)*.

CHINESE ROBES & EMBROIDERY. The textile art of China is often a tour de force of skill and nowhere more so than in its embroidery. Here again, the individual motifs are worth examining for design approaches.

LEFT. Embroidered Chinese picture, early 18th Century. Such panels — with superb stitchery and incredibly subtle gradations of color — were made for export to the West. *V & A — FD1633 (T181–1948).*

ABOVE. Detail of embroidered twelve-symbol marriage robe, 19th Century. *V & A — FG1781 (T253–1907).*

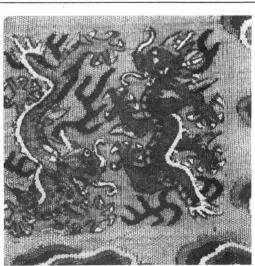

BELOW LEFT. Child's embroidered bag, Ch'ing period (1644–1912). *V & A —- M1981 (T122 to C–1948).*

TOP. Chinese Imperial hunting robe, K'ang Hsi (1662–1722). *V & A — G823 (T186–1948).*

BOTTOM, LEFT TO RIGHT. Three details from a twelve-symbol Chinese robe of woven silk. Ch'ien Ling period, 18th Century. Shown are the Moon (Hare), Paired Dragons, and Pheasant. *V & A — K1820 (T214–1948).*

IMPORTANT LACE COLLECTIONS. The largest collection of lace in the UK/Ireland is held by the V & A with some 2,500 pieces. Next comes Nottingham with about 2,000 pieces. Liverpool ranks third with perhaps 1,000 pieces, followed by Royal Scottish (800), Whitworth (500), and Cecil Higgins (400). Smaller but interesting collections are owned by the following: Gallery of English Costume (200), National Museum of Ireland (NMI), Ulster Museum (170), Ulster Folk Museum, Burrell Collection (120), Strangers' Hall, Bankfield Museum, Fitzwilliam (60), British Museum (fans), and Museum of London (costume). Mention should also be made here of three collections

not listed elsewhere in this volume and noted chiefly for their lace collections: the museums at Luton and York and the collection at Gawthorpe Hall (near Burnley, Lancs.) assembled by Rachel Kay-Suttleworth.

TOP LEFT. Punto in aria, 1640. *NMI — 157–1903.* TOP RIGHT. Point d'Argentan, 1730. *NMI — 47–1933.* BOTTOM LEFT. Point de France, 17th Century. *V & A — FG966 (T36B–1949).* MIDDLE RIGHT. Gros Point, Venice, 17th Century. *Fitzwilliam — 4378 (T3–1964).* BOTTOM RIGHT. Lacis cloth. Italy, 17th Century. *Royal Scottish — 1870.52.3.*

THE PATTERNS OF LACE. The intricate structures of lace often create the effect of rare jewels or finely chased silver engravings. As such, they offer design themes for other types of textiles, especially prints, where the jewellike forms can be interpreted in pigment — white traceries on a jet ground.

TOP LEFT. Collar of Irish crochet, c. 1850. *National Museum of Ireland — 431–1909.*

TOP RIGHT. Possibly Swiss, 1895–1900. *V & A — FG896 (T179–1962)*.

BOTTOM LEFT. Youghal needlepoint lace, 1880. *National Museum of Ireland — 718–1912.*

BOTTOM RIGHT. French Point d'Alençon. First half of 19th Century. *V & A — FG1067 (31–18880)*.

FAR RIGHT. Brussels needlepoint lace shown at Chicago Exhibit, 1893. *V & A — GX5559 (T366–1970)*.

19–20TH-CENTURY LACE. An ancient skill, still practiced today as it was in the 16th Century.

TOP LEFT. Tabernacle veil of Irish Kenmare needlepoint lace. It was made in 1911 at St. Care's Convent in Kenmare, Co. Kerry. The convent has a collection of lace. *National Museum of Ireland — 419–1911.*

BOTTOM LEFT. Border and square of Irish tatting, 1850–1880. *Nat. Mus. of Ireland — 781–1880; 981–1891.*

TOP RIGHT. Bag cover of cotton netting. Palestinian, 20th Century. *Royal Scottish — 1962.1202.*

BOTTOM RIGHT. Table mat of cotton lace made in Czechoslovakia, 1935–1940. The piece is approximately two feet in diameter. *Royal Scottish Museum — 1962.1164. Needlework Development Scheme Bequest.*

FAR RIGHT, TOP. Design for fan cover of Irish Carrickmacross lace, 1914. *Nat. Mus. of Ireland.*

FAR RIGHT, BOTTOM. English bobbin lace, Honiton, second half 19th Century. *V & A — FG1065 (T15 1963).*

SPITALFIELDS SILKS — 18TH CENTURY. The second and third quarters of the 18th Century were the most flourishing years for English silk weaving. Its chief center was in Spitalfields, then a hamlet just outside the walls of London. It produced plain silks, mixtures of silk with linen or wool, black silk, gauze, and elaborately figured or flowered silks, whose changing designs set the fashion from season to season.

FAR LEFT. Spitalfields brocaded silk with typical floral design. *V & A — L1519 (723–1905)*.

LEFT TOP. Design no. 173 by Anna Maria Garthwaite for Spitalfields silk, 1731. *V & A — Z2323 (5972.3)*.

LEFT BOTTOM. Another Garthwaite Spitalfields design on paper, dated c. 1726. *V & A — TD947 (5973.8)*.

RIGHT TOP. English brocaded dress silk with chenille thread, c. 1733. *V & A — GA296 (T9+A–1971)*.

RIGHT BOTTOM. English woven silk with stylized floral motifs, 1729–30. *V & A — K1125 (T15–1951)*.

FAR RIGHT. English or Dutch woven silk with dark ground, c. 1730–32. *V & A — Z2468 (Circ 173A–1917)*.

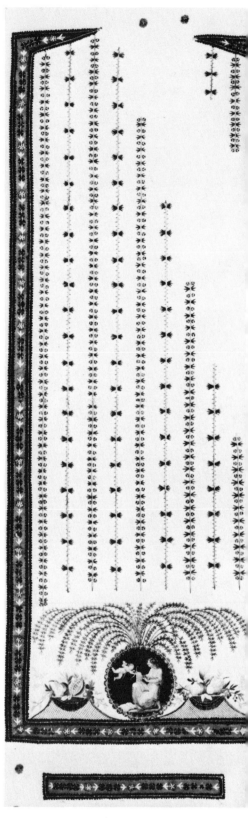

EMBROIDERY COLLECTIONS. Historic embroidery is often neglected as a source of contemporary textile design, perhaps because it generally shows no design repeat and is therefore more difficult to adapt than woven or printed textiles. But embroidery can be a most rewarding source of textile design ideas. It is perhaps the most ancient and least technological way of decorating a fabric. Requiring only a needle and thread, it abounds in personal expression which is rooted in time and place. Moreover, the source material is plentiful. Most museums in the U.K. and Ireland have substantial embroidery collections. The largest and most varied are those in the V & A, the Gallery of

English Costume, the Whitworth, the Royal Scottish, the Burrell, the Ulster Folk, the Merseyside, and the Nottingham. The variety of ideas in these collections is illustrated by the diverse pieces shown here and on the following two pages.

LEFT. Italian chasuble, c. 1725. *Royal Scot. — 1945.4571.* CENTER. English waistcoat fronts, c. 1790. *Mus. of London — 51.21.* RIGHT. Dutch sampler, 18th *Century V & A — 81761 (T11–1937).*

ENGLISH EMBROIDERY — 18TH CENTURY

ABOVE. Detail of embroidered English coverlet with outline stitching as overall background patterning. It was made with silk thread on a linen cloth in the mid–18th Century. *V & A–GX5555 (T381–1970)*.

TOP LEFT. Late 18th-Century embroidered map of "the farm called Arnolds" in Essex. The ground is wool canvas. The thread is silk and chenille. *V & A — M2400 (T65–1954)*.

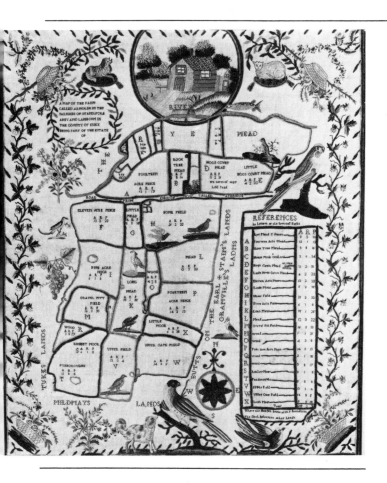

TOP RIGHT. Elaborate embroidery on a man's coat, c. 1720. *Bath Museum of Costume (no acc. no.).*

BOTTOM LEFT. English chair seat, embroidered in silk, 18th Century. *V & A — GA418 (T474–1970).*

BOTTOM RIGHT. English stumpwork panel. Scenes from the story of David and Bathsheba. Dated 1700. Silk and metal threads on a silk ground. Also mica, beads, coral, feathers, wire. Stitches: buttonhole, couching, cross, hollie point, long, short, satin, stem, French knot. *Fitzwilliam — K3013 (T5–1954). Utting Bequest.*

FRENCH WOVEN SILKS — 18TH CENTURY. During the 18th Century, French silk weaving, based in Lyon, became world renowned for its skill and elegance. A few examples are shown here.

FAR LEFT. ''Flame Stitch'' silk hanging woven by Pierre Maille, 1732–40. *V & A — FH1730 (T204–1960)*.

LEFT TOP. French woven silk from the first quarter of the 18th Century. *V & A — X5 (593–1896)*.

LEFT BOTTOM. French brocaded silk woven about 1735, possibly in Tours. *V & A — Y543 (600–1896)*.

RIGHT TOP. French silk furnishings panel, woven in the late 18th Century. *V & A — T135–1927.*

RIGHT BOTTOM. A French "Bizarre" design in brocaded silk damask, 1700–1705. *V & A — P858 (T17–1956).*

FAR RIGHT. French brocaded silk, designed by Philippe de Lasalle (1723–1803), most famous of 18th-Century French designers, and woven in Lyon by Camille Peinon about 1770. *V & A — L1849 (T187–1931).*

18TH-CENTURY MISCELLANY — WOVENS

LEFT. A sharply etched Italian silk cloth woven in the first quarter of the 18th Century. This is a large-scale design with a repeat of about 30 inches. *V & A — G5209 (447+A–1906).*

RIGHT. Woven velvet from Turkey, 18–19th Century. *V & A — 66228 (36-1878).*

LEFT. Length of silk brocade made in Moscow (U.S.S.R.) during the first half of the 18th Century. The design is large in scale with a repeat of about 20 inches. *Royal Scottish Museum — 1930–341.*

RIGHT. Italian velvet made in Genoa, first quarter of the 18th Century. *V & A — 79551 (340–1891).*

18TH-CENTURY TEXTILE PRINTS

LEFT. The famous "Volunteer" copperplate print made in 1783 by Harpur & Cunningham of Leixlip, Ireland. It should be noted that the first copperplate prints came from Ireland in 1752. *National Museum of Ireland.*

RIGHT. German peasant print from Bavaria dating from the middle of the 18th Century. It was made by woodblock and printed on a linen ground. *V & A — 53247 (1667–1899).*

TOP. 18th-Century French printed cotton with a design much influenced by the imported "Indiennes" designs so popular in France at that time. *V & A — E361 (T280–1919).*

BOTTOM. French toile made in Nantes, 1785. It depicts "Cherbourg." *V & A — 77239 (T465-1919).*

RIGHT. English copperplate print by Robert Jones of Old Ford, 1761. *V & A — 36243 (442-1897).*

INDIA'S STORY-TELLING TEXTILES. Among the most fascinating of India's textiles are those which illustrate its folk legends and history. Three such pieces are shown here.

BELOW. Temple curtain of painted cotton from Madura, Madras, 18th Century. *V & A — L488 (IM29–1911)*.

TOP RIGHT. An 18th Century *rumal* or kerchief of muslin embroidered with silk. It comes from Chamba, the Himalayan region in India, and illustrates an erotic phase in the legendary life of Krishna — his dance with the Gopis, wives of the cowherds. *V & A — G1023 (IS2098–1883).*

BOTTOM RIGHT. Section of an embroidered cotton hanging over 32 feet long, also from 18th-Century Chamba. It illustrates a battle described in the Hindu national epic, Mahabharata. *V & A — 18434 (IS1185–1883).*

PAINTED COTTONS OF INDIA — 18TH CENTURY. The "painted" cottons of India were made by a method not unlike that of batik printing — that is, they were painted with a mordant and resist-dyed. It is this type we find abundantly in museum collections, since they were valuable and generally made for export. Other and less valuable Indian cottons were block printed and dyed, but fewer of these have survived, since they were expendable. In both cases the Indian fabrics were much faster in color than European prints of the 17th and 18th Centuries. The designs were obviously influenced by Persian painting, as can be seen here.

LEFT. Section of painted-and-dyed cotton bedspread, dated c. 1740. *V & A — H1116 (IS42–1950)*.

TOP. Painted-and-dyed cotton from the Coromandel coast, 18th Century. *V & A — H1233 (IS48a–1950)*.

BOTTOM. Enlarged detail of bedspread on the left. Each pictorial vignette is filled with textile designs. The whole piece is an archive of Indian motifs and patterns. *V & A — H1115 (IS42–1950)*.

THE INDIAN PALAMPORE — 18TH CENTURY. The textile most often associated with 18th-Century India is the *palampore* — a bed covering. It was traditionally painted and dyed by skilled cotton painters, and its most representative design was the flowering tree derived from Persian painting. As export products to European markets these textiles had their greatest vogue during the first quarter of the 18th Century, but they continued well into the century until copperplate printing made them obsolete. Not all such covers or hangings used the flowering tree design, as can be seen from these examples.

FAR LEFT. Painted–and–dyed cotton palampore, N. Deccan, late 18th Century. *V & A — K1482 (IS51–1952)*.

LEFT. Section of printed floor spread, Haiderabad, early 18th Century. *V & A — Z975 (IM69–1927)*.

RIGHT. Painted-and-dyed cotton palampore, 17–18th Century. *V & A — H1130 (IS31-1950)*.

FAR RIGHT. Printed palampore from Masulipatam, 18th Century. *V & A — 1176 (64–1904)*.

GREEK ISLAND EMBROIDERY — 17–18TH CENTURY. One of the world's largest collections of Greek Island embroidery is owned by the V & A with over 800 pieces. Nothing else comparable exists in the UK/Ireland, but eight other museums own good and representative collections. The most important are those at Merseyside, the Whitworth, Newcastle (Laing Gallery), the Fitzwilliam, and the Royal Scottish. There are also three smaller collections at the Gallery of English Costume, the Museum of Mankind, and the National Museum of Ireland. The examples shown here illustrate the variety of these designs.

FACING PAGE: LEFT. Cushion cover, Cyclades, 18th Century. *V & A — FG1688 (T635–1950)*. RIGHT. Linen bed curtain, Rhodes, 18th Century. *Royal Scottish — (1936.392)*. BOTTOM. Skirt border, Crete, 17–18th Century. *V & A — GX4441 (T215–1929)*. THIS PAGE: LEFT. Apron from Crete, embroidered in the 17–18th Century. *V & A — GX4442 (T636–1950)*. RIGHT. Embroidered band from the Cyclades Islands, 17–18th Century. *V & A — 82083 (T121-1939)*. BOTTOM. Embroidered skirt border, from Crete, 18th Century. *V & A — GX4444 (2048–1876)*. Many of these embroideries were done in silk thread on a linen cloth.

SWEDISH PEASANT WEAVING — SKÅNE. The two textiles reproduced above were both woven in Skåne, one of Sweden's southern coastal provinces, in the late 18th or early 19th Century. The peasant designs of Skåne have their own distinctive quality, and the two shown here are representative of the culture.

TOP. A carriage cushion cover in a tapestry weave known as *Flamsk vävnad* or "Flemish weaving." This was a peasant adaptation of the elaborate Flemish tapestries commissioned for the royal palace by King Gustav Vasa in

1540. *V & A — Z1904 (Circ 149–1962)*. BOTTOM. Another cushion cover in the "rölakan" weave, which is made on a horizontal warp and has geometric motifs. *V & A — R1131 (T77-1913)*.

BAVARIAN WOVEN SILK. The handsome design above might have been made by William Morris or C. F. A. Voysey. It has the sculptural quality of their designs. But it is not English. It was made in Bavaria, 1870–73, and is silk, woven with a jacquard attachment. *V & A — FE2288 (529-1874)*.

19TH-CENTURY WEAVING — MOROCCO, SWEDEN, NORTH AFRICA

LEFT. A length of woven silk from Morocco, 19th Century. *V & A — M1632 (733–1894).*

CENTER. Another length of woven silk from Morocco, 18–19th Century. *V & A — M1639 (T81–1910).*

170

FACING PAGE, RIGHT. Cushion cover in tapestry weave from Skåne province in southern Sweden, early 19th Century. It was made with colored wools on a linen warp. *V & A — R1132 (T78-1913).*

ABOVE. Woven kilim carpet from N. Africa, 19th Century. *V & A — GA1575 (T206–1928).*

CAUCASUS. The intricate and heavily covered design below is not a woven carpet but an embroidered cover made in the Caucasus during the late 18th or early 19th Century. *V & A — GA2314 (401–1906).*

IRAN. TOP RIGHT. A Turcoman camel trapping from the Yomut tribe of N.E. Iran. It was made in the early part of this century and was constructed by a carpet technique of Turkish knots in wool yarns on a wool warp. This type of hanging is used at festivals and weddings. Dimensions are 29¼ x 43½ inches. Not shown is a 9-inch fringe of wool

tassels. One of a pair. *Whitworth — 3171a/8 (T15163).*

BOTTOM. From the same source as the piece above comes this camel flank hanging made by embroidery and patchwork. The base fabric is flannel, and the reverse side has a cotton print lining. Also not shown in this photograph is a long fringe made out of silk and cotton scraps. Size of the hanging is 22 x 40½ inches without the fringe. It is one in a set of three similar hangings. *Whitworth — 3172a/7 (T15170b).*

IKAT — CENTRAL ASIA — 19TH CENTURY. The ikat technique of decorating a fabric by tie-dyeing the yarns before weaving was a traditional textile process used in several parts of the world. Most often only the warp yarns were tie-dyed, but in double ikats both the warp and weft yarns were so treated. In both cases the tie-dyeing was engineered to create a preplanned pattern in the finished cloth. We often associate ikats with Indonesia or Japan. Less well known and often more dramatic are the ikats from Central Asia.

LEFT. Door curtain in silk ikat from Persia (Iran), 19th Century. *V & A — Q1527 (993–1886)*.

CENTER. Silk/cotton ikat from Yarkand in W. China (Turcoman), 19th Century. *V & A — Q1522 (IS1389–1883)*.

RIGHT. Silk/cotton ikat, also from Yarkand, 19th Century. *V & A — Q1525 (IS2121–1883)*.

IKAT — INDONESIA — 19–20TH CENTURY. The three textiles reproduced here illustrate how different the ikats of Indonesia are from those of Central Asia. Within the different ikat-producing regions of Indonesia there are also substantial differences in design. Even on the little Indonesian island of Sumba — now internationally famous for its ikats — there are differences between the designs made on different parts of the island, as well as between the fabrics made for export and those reserved for local ceremonial use. This indicates how rich a source of design ideas is the whole ikat field.

LEFT. Cotton-warp ikat from the Celebes Islands, c. 1900. *V & A — FG1181 (IS19–1960)*.

CENTER. A contemporary shroud cloth from the Celebes Islands. *V & A — FG1188 (IS60–1961)*.

RIGHT. Man's single-ikat shoulder cloth, probably E. Sumba, c. 1900. *V & A — FG1187 (IS59–1961)*.

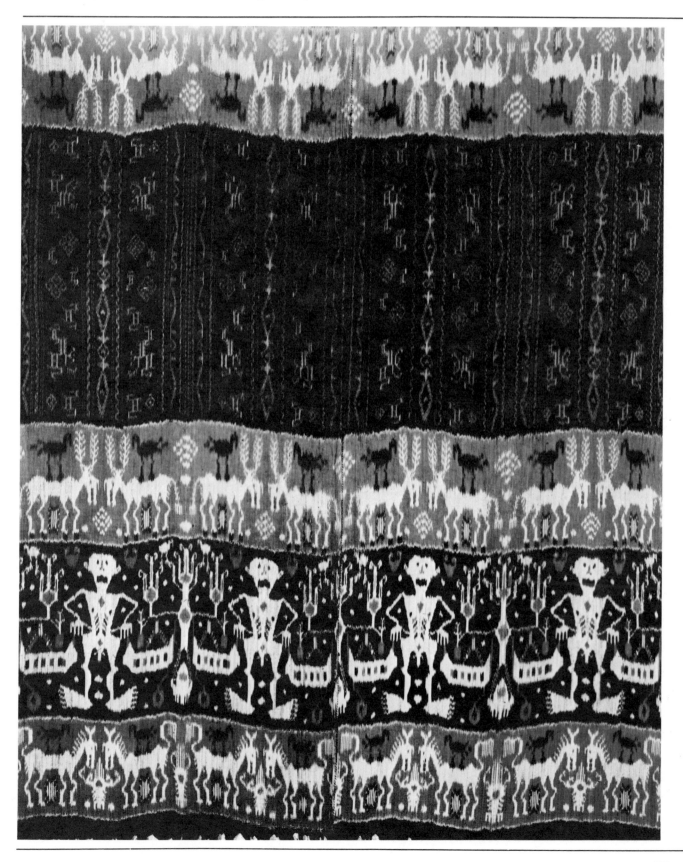

BATIK — JAVA — 19–20TH CENTURY — I. The batiks of Java emerge from a distinctive tradition of decorative art which goes back to the 13th Century and is Hindu in origin. They have a character very much their own, and this is apparent in the examples shown here, all chosen from the fine collection of over 100 Javanese batiks in the Indian Section of the V & A. (See V & A book titled "Batiks.")

BELOW. Cotton sarong in brown and indigo, Central Java, late 19th Century. *V & A — FD2476 (IM268–1921).*

TOP. Cotton shoulder cloth (slendang) with wax applied by copper blocks (tjap). Colors are indigo and light brown on a white ground. Central Java, 19–20th Century. *V & A — FG694 (IS144–1964)*.

BOTTOM. Section of silk shoulder cloth. N. Java coast, c. 1920. *V & A — X531 (IS28–1960)*.

RIGHT. Cotton sarong, red and black. N. Java, late 19th Century. *V & A — FG690 (IS65–1961)*.

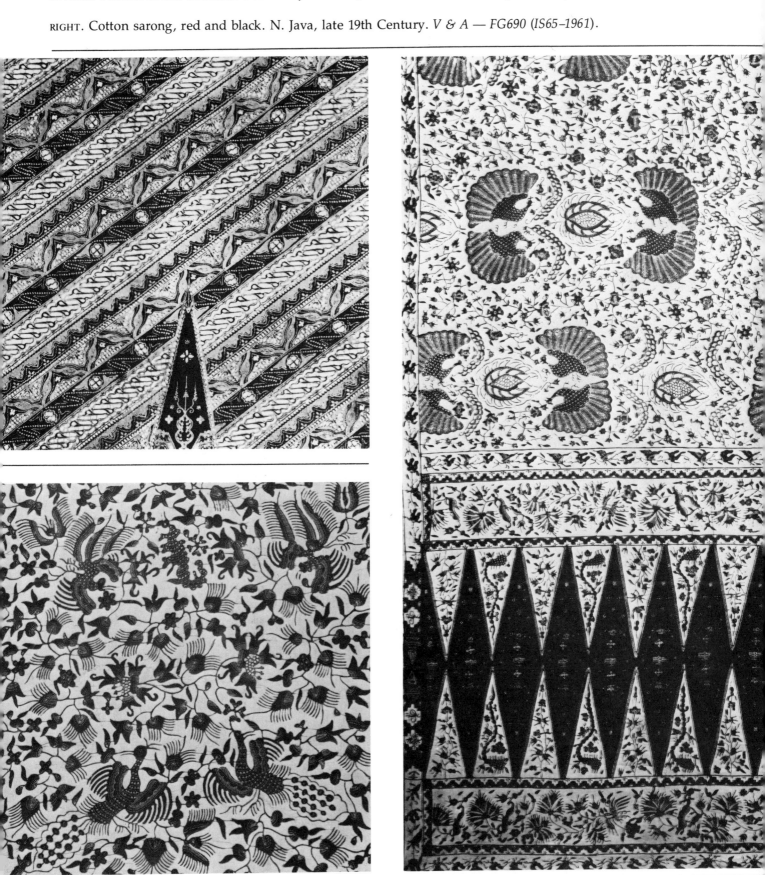

JAVANESE BATIKS — II

ABOVE. Section of cotton sarong from E. Java, late 19th Century. The design was applied by both wax pen (tjanting) and copper blocks. Colors are indigo, brown, and red. *V & A — FD2483 (IS64–1961)*.

TOP LEFT. Man's cotton cloth (kain pandjang), C. Java, late 19th Century. *V & A — X541 (IM267–1921)*.

TOP RIGHT. Cotton cloth, indigo and light brown. C. Java, 20th Century. *V & A — FG699 (IS146–1964)*.

BOTTOM LEFT. Cotton skirt cloth, fish-scale design. C. Java, 20th Century. *V & A — FG701 (IS172–1964)*.

BOTTOM RIGHT. Indigo and brown batik on white ground. C. Java, c. 1930. *V & A — X543 (IS31–1960)*.

JAVANESE BATIKS — III

TOP LEFT. Head cloth in cotton batik. Central Java, c. 1920. *V & A — X529 (IS26–1960)*.

TOP RIGHT. Handkerchief batik from Java. Early 20th Century. *Museum of Mankind — 50010 (1923-4-10-19)*.

BOTTOM. Shadow puppet figures (called *waygang*) are colored brown and white on an indigo ground. This batik was made in Central Java in the late 19th century. *V & A — FG1854 (T95–1959).*

ABOVE. Batik in red, green, blue, brown. N. Java, 20th Century. *Museum of Mankind — 50012 (1934–3–7–87).*

JAPAN — RESIST-DYED COTTONS — 19TH CENTURY

Resist-dyed cottons — chiefly indigo and white — are found in most folk cultures from Central Europe to Africa and the Far East. Those of Japan have a character of their own. Using a rice-paste resist, the design was applied either by stencil or by hand painting. Shown below is a superb example of the resist technique used for a coverlet. Japan, 19th Century. *V & A — GA13 (T199–1964).*

JAPAN — EMBROIDERY — 19TH CENTURY

There are magnificent examples of embroidery art from many cultures at the V & A, but to us the most impressive are those exhibited in the Far East study hall (Room 98). Among these none is more arresting than the 19th-Century Japanese embroidery reproduced here. It is a tour de force of skill and articulation, in silver-colored silk on a deep navy-blue satin ground. *V & A — 69554 (T94–1927).*

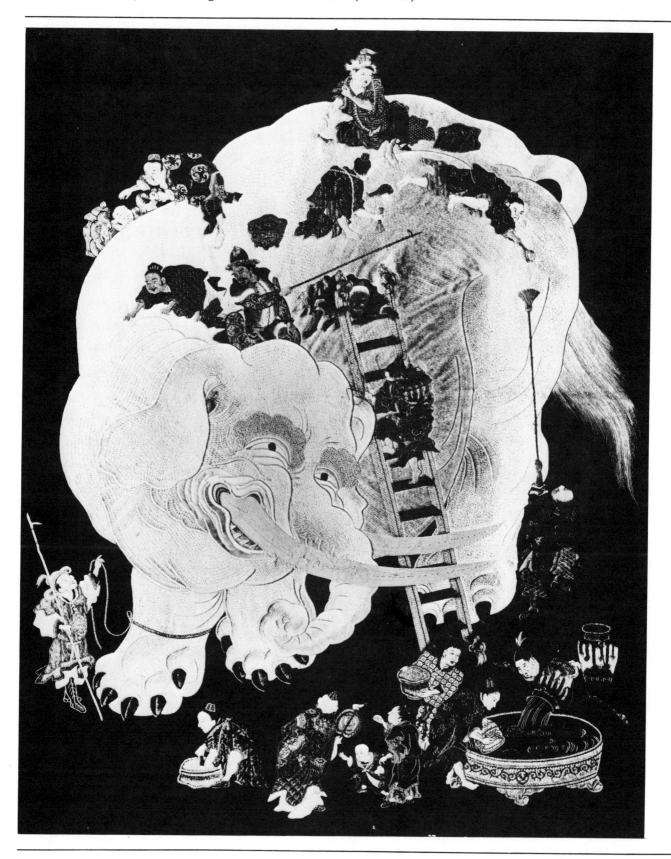

JAPAN — 19TH-CENTURY MISCELLANY

ABOVE. Japanese embroidery in gold-colored silk, 18–19th Century. *V & A — Q1724 (T20–1923)*.

RIGHT. Resist-dyed cotton with embroidery. Japan, 19th Century. *V & A — GA11 (T203–1964)*.

FAR RIGHT, TOP. A 19th-Century Japanese folk textile made by the ikat technique known as *kasuri* and

e-gasuri, which means "picture kasuri." This whole category of Japanese folk textile art is a valuable source for contemporary print design, since it is easily adapted. *V & A — GA3 (T128–1968).*

FAR RIGHT, BOTTOM. A 19th-Century appliqué robe of the Ainu people who inhabit the northernmost islands of Japan. Appliqué work is characteristic of the Ainu culture, which is thought of as "primitive" but seems both sophisticated and abstract to 20th-Century eyes. *V & A — FF1091 (T99–1963).*

BELOW. Woman's woven-silk marriage cloth. India, 19th Century. *V & A — G991 (IS97–1948).*

TOP LEFT. Block-printed cotton from Trichinopoly, 19th Century. *V & A — L481 (IS2899–1883).*

TOP RIGHT. Woven silk/cotton sari from Bangalore, 19th Century. *V & A — P1340 (IS441B).*

BOTTOM LEFT. Cutch embroidery with mirror inserts. Bombay, 19th Century. *V & A — Y80 (IM274–1920).*

BOTTOM RIGHT. Indian tie-dyed cloth, second half of 19th Century. *Horniman — 2301.*

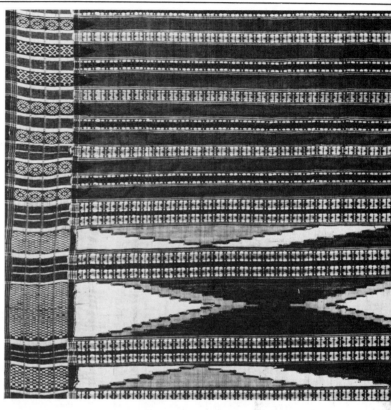
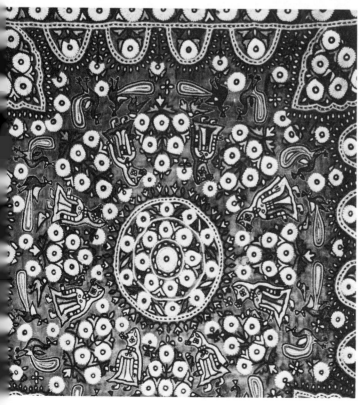

INDIA — 19TH-CENTURY MISCELLANY — II

TOP LEFT. Embroidered cotton hanging, Gujarat, W. India. Contemporary. *V & A — FJ1750 (IS18–1967)*.

TOP RIGHT. Cotton patchwork with embroidery. Kathiawar, 19th Century. *Royal Scottish — 1962.1209.*

BOTTOM. Appliqué cotton hanging from Burma, 19th Century. *V & A — X1978 (IS8–1952)*.

FAR RIGHT. A painted-and-dyed cotton tablecloth from the Masulipatam region of India. It was made in the late 18th or early 19th Century. *V & A — Z1185 (IS25–1950)*.

INDIA — KASHMIR SHAWLS — 19TH CENTURY

TOP. Corner detail of Kashmir shawl, loom woven and finished by hand with a needle. Made about 1865. Many shawls from Kashmir were produced in this manner. *V & A — GA3385 (IS8–1954)*.

BOTTOM. Loom-woven Kashmir shawl made about 1830. *V & A — M1566 (IS2000–1883)*.

TOP LEFT. Shawl used as curtain. Made in Amritsar, Punjab, c. 1830. *V & A — M283 (IM14–1933)*.

TOP RIGHT. Wool Kashmir shawl embroidered with white silk, 19th Century. *Royal Scottish — 1962–1211*.

BOTTOM LEFT. Woven Kashmir scarf with outline embroidery, c. 1865. *V & A — M284 (IS0804)*.

BOTTOM RIGHT. Loom-woven Kashmir shawl of wool, 19th Century. *V & A — M705 (IS2081a–1883)*.

ENGLAND — NORWICH SHAWLS — 19TH CENTURY

Four examples of Norwich shawls, all from *Strangers' Hall Museum*. TOP LEFT. Shawl woven in 1827. TOP RIGHT. A "darned" shawl counterpane, c. 1800. In the first loom-woven shawls the decoration was "darned" or embroidered by hand. On loan from The National Trust, Eastern Area, Blickling, Norfolk. BOTTOM LEFT. Silk shawl woven by Clabburn, Sons & Crisp, 1863. BOTTOM RIGHT. Wool shawl by Willett & Co., c. 1850.

SCOTLAND — PAISLEY SHAWLS — 19TH CENTURY

Two examples of the Paisley product which dominated the industry during most of the 19th Century.

LEFT. Woven in wool/cotton about 1860. Size is 139 x 63½ inches. *Royal Scottish Museum — 1958.207.*

RIGHT. Woven in wool/silk, c. 1860. Size is 154 x 62½ inches. *Royal Scottish — 1925.114. Hendry Bequest.*

FRANCE — LYON SHAWLS — 19TH CENTURY

The European vogue for "imitation Oriental shawls" lasted longer than most fashion trends. It began at the turn of the 19th Century and faded only when the crinoline (which supported it) began to be displaced in the 1870s. During that long period the town of Paisley in Scotland became the most important shawl resource in the West, but its close competitor was Lyon in France — the leading center for Jacquard silk weaving during this period.

French weavers applied all their extraordinary skills to the design and manufacture of these shawls, and it was generally conceded in the market that their products had an edge over those of Paisley. The quality and detail of the French shawls is demonstrated in these examples.

LEFT & CENTER. Section and details of a French shawl woven about 1840. *V & A — GA2309 (T189–1960)*.

RIGHT. French version of the traditional "pine" motif in a shawl, c. 1855. *V & A — M274 (T37–1938)*.

BRITISH PATCHWORK QUILTS

The patchwork quilt is traditionally associated with Colonial America. But the patchwork and appliqué quilt was made in Britain, too, and probably also for economic reasons, at least at first. Later, these quilts became something of a fashion, and manufacturers produced special fabrics for this purpose — floral centerpieces printed by the yard, ready to be cut out and appliquéd. Two such pieces are shown here.

LEFT. English patchwork quilt with printed centerpiece, made in 1810. *V & A — 82516 (T181–1941).*
TOP LEFT. English patchwork of printed cottons, c. 1837. 78 x 68 inches. *V & A — 68554 (T172–1922).*
TOP RIGHT. Irish "mosaic" patchwork from Ballywattick, 19th Century. *Ulster Folk Museum — L341/3.*
BOTTOM LEFT. English patchwork with printed centerpiece, 19th Century. *V & A — 76145 (T17–1924).*
BOTTOM RIGHT. Scottish "Log Cabin" patchwork, 1884. *Royal Scottish Museum — 1961.419. Dykes Bequest.*

BRITISH APPLIQUÉ & PATCHWORK

In England the term "patchwork" refers to pieces of cloth sewn together to form a cover. When pieces are sewn on top of a cover to form a design, it is called "appliqué." Patchwork was made as early as 1700.

LEFT. English appliqué design, c. 1851. The floral bouquet was a printed centerpiece. The standing figures were copied from the "Greek Slave" sculpture by Hiram Powers. *V & A — S356 (T86–1957)*.

LEFT. English silk brocatelle by Daniel Walters & Sons, c. 1862. *V & A — L1268 (Circ 229–1955)*.

RIGHT. English linen-damask napkin, early 19th Century. *V & A — GX4021 (T66–1955)*.

TOP LEFT. English damask by Bailey & Jackson, Spitalfields, 1839–46. *V & A — L1515 (483–1897)*.

BOTTOM LEFT. Detail of English silk-damask curtain woven in the 1820s. *V & A — V1915 (T3–1950)*.

RIGHT. French home-furnishings fabric woven in the early 19th Century. *V & A — 66197 (T340–1913)*.

ENGLISH WOVEN RIBBONS — 19TH CENTURY

In their day the decorative silk ribbons of Coventry were as famous and as skillfully woven as the shawls of Paisley. For contemporary designers they are a rewarding source of ideas with an extremely wide range of patterns and motifs. They are also a revealing barometer of fashion and color trends during the mid-19th Century. And as for Coventry's picture ribbons, they should be most interesting to print designers.

TOP. Pages from a ribbon sample book of the 1860s, now owned by the *Bath Museum of Costume.*

BOTTOM. "The Last Lap," silk picture ribbon by Thos. Stevens, Coventry, 1870–80. *V & A — S2041 (T58–1958).*

LEFT. Silk Coventry ribbon shown in 1862 Exhibition. *V & A — Y193 (T90–1957). Camb. U. Lib. Bequest.*

RIGHT. Famous Coventry ribbon by M. Clack shown at the 1851 Exhibition. *V & A — S2040 (T29–1947).*

ENGLISH EMBROIDERY — 19TH CENTURY

Many trends enlivened the embroidery scene in 19th-Century England — from Berlin woolwork to art needlework (under the influence of William Morris) in the later years of the century.

LEFT. Early 19th-Century blotter cover, silk embroidery on velvet. *V & A — FE1123 (T399–1910)*.

TOP LEFT. Berlin woolwork fire screen from Belfast, 1880. Berlin woolwork was so named because the first patterns (in color on squared paper) were issued by a Berlin publisher. *Ulster Folk Museum — L692/3.*

TOP RIGHT. Embroidered panel by Lewis F. Day, 1890. *Gallery of English Costume — 3923 (1929–338/2).*

BOTTOM. Section of art-needlework panel by Miss E. D. Bradby, 1899. *V & A — FG441 (T270–1927).*

ENGLISH & FRENCH PRINTS — 19TH CENTURY

TOP LEFT. Detail of English dress print, 1853–6. *Gallery of English Costume — 2313 (1947–2332).*

TOP RIGHT. English print on striped muslin, 1822–5. *Gallery of English Costume — 2107 (1947–1782).*

BOTTOM LEFT. English print made in 1835–40. *V & A — FD1146 (T53–1964). Baker Bequest.*

BOTTOM RIGHT. Mid-19th-Century English print with Chinoiserie figure. *V & A — FD1145 (T52–1964).*

TOP LEFT. French block-printed cotton with stippled ground, early 19th Century. *V & A — J12 (159–1919).*

TOP RIGHT. English "toile" in the Chinoiserie style, 1820–25. *V & A — FD1152 (T64–1964). Baker Bequest.*

BOTTOM. French cotton Toile de Jouy titled "Scènes Pompèiennes." It was designed by J. B. Huet, most famous of the artists at the Oberkampf printworks. Early 19th Century. *V & A — 77240 (T329–1919).*

THE DESIGNS OF WILLIAM MORRIS — ENGLISH, LATE 19TH CENTURY

The designs of William Morris have withstood the test of time, and many of them were made almost a hundred years ago. They are sharply etched, crisp, beautifully composed, and still satisfying to the contemporary eye. In black-and-white reproduction the graphic qualities of the designs are emphasized. Designers should also be aware that the color ways are subtle and unusual. Much can be learned from them even today.

FAR LEFT. The "Snakehead" chintz, a print cloth designed by Morris in 1877. *V & A — L2320 (T37–1919)*.
TOP LEFT. The "Yare" chintz, a hand-blocked home-furnishings fabric by Morris. *William Morris Gallery*.
TOP RIGHT. The "Compton" chintz, another of the 122 printed textiles owned by the *William Morris Gallery*.
BOTTOM LEFT. The "Eyebright" design, made in 1883. Hand-blocked cotton. *V & A — L1956 (Circ 420–1953)*.
BOTTOM RIGHT. The "Rose & Lilly" design, woven in silk and wool. *William Morris Gallery*.

ENGLISH NAME DESIGNERS — LATE 19TH CENTURY — I

The Good Design movement in Great Britain during the latter part of the 19th Century had William Morris as its most articulate spokesman, but he was not alone. A number of other artist/designers and textile producers were equally dedicated to the cause of improving British design. Many of these people worked with Morris and were influenced by him. Their work reveals the same elegance and uncluttered quality.

TOP LEFT. "Saladin," an English cotton print by C. F. A. Voysey, c. 1897. *V & A — Q823 (T29–1953)*.

TOP RIGHT. "Tulip," a wool tapestry weave by J. H. Dearle, c. 1890. *V & A — M72 (T110–1953)*.

BOTTOM LEFT. Upholstery fabric woven by Alexander Morton & Co. in the 1890s. *Whitworth — A839 (11893)*.

BOTTOM RIGHT. Printed cotton by Lewis F. Day for Turnbull & Stockdale, 1890s. *Whitworth — A833 (10348)*.

FAR RIGHT. "Marlboro," silk damask by Owen Jones for Warners Ltd., 1872. *V & A — GX3509 (T159–1972)*.

ENGLISH NAME DESIGNERS — LATE 19TH CENTURY — II

TOP LEFT. Silk damask for 1897 Diamond Jubilee, by the Benj. Warner firm. *V & A — GX3619 (T176–1972).*
TOP RIGHT. "Evenlode" chintz, a printed fabric designed by William Morris. *William Morris Gallery.*
BOTTOM LEFT. "Nizam," a woven designed by Owen Jones for Warner, 1870. *V & A — K846 (T94D–1930).*
BOTTOM RIGHT. Block-print cotton by Lindsay Butterfield for Wardle of Leek, 1895. *Whitworth — A79 (10184).*

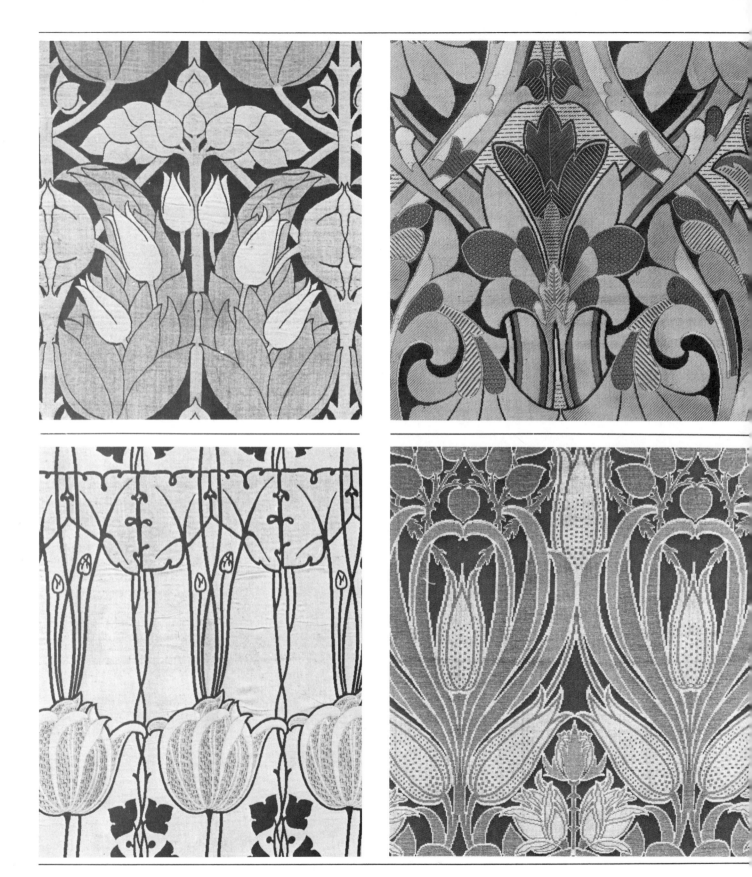

TOP LEFT. "Omar," reversible woven by Harrison Townsend for Morton & Co., c. 1900. *Whitworth — A837 (11832)*.

TOP RIGHT. Woven silk by Owen Jones for Warner, 1870–80. *V & A — L1502 (T94A–1930)*.

BOTTOM LEFT. Reversible woven, probably by Voysey, for Morton & Co., 1890s. *Whitworth — A835 (11889)*.

BOTTOM RIGHT. "Malmsley," woven probably by Voysey for Morton, c. 1899. *Whitworth — A843 (11860)*.

ENGLISH NAME DESIGNERS — LATE 19TH CENTURY — III

LEFT. "The Owl," a woven fabric designed by C. F. A. Voysey in 1897. *V & A — Q830 (T11–1953).*

TOP LEFT. "Powdered" chintz, a Morris design originally made for wallpaper. *William Morris Gallery.*

TOP RIGHT. "Cherwell," a Morris print on velveteen, designed about 1884. *William Morris Gallery.*

BOTTOM LEFT. "Brocatel," a silk brocatelle designed by Morris about 1888. *V & A — L1945 (Circ 86–1953).*

BOTTOM RIGHT. Block-printed cotton by Walter Crane for Birch Gibson, 1901. *Whitworth — A852 (11728).*

PEASANT EMBROIDERY — 19–20TH CENTURY. The embroideries on these pages all belong to the Royal Scottish Museum. They are part of a large needlework collection given to the museum by the Needlework Development Scheme, which did much to encourage experimentation with embroidery in the country's art schools.

ABOVE. Enlarged detail and complete man's robe from Damascus, Syria, 19–20th Century. The robe is cotton. The embroidery is done with silk in needle weaving and stem stitch. *Royal Scottish Museum — 1962.1200.*

LEFT. Cotton embroidery from N. Africa, 19–20th Century, 16½ x 8¼ inches. *Royal Scottish — 1962.1243.*

TOP RIGHT. Embroidered linen table mat, Yugoslavia, c. 1935, 15 x 12 inches. *Royal Scottish — 1963.1182.*

BOTTOM RIGHT. Mexican panel, wool embroidery, 1935–40, 23 x 18 inches. *Royal Scottish — 1962.1253.*

TAPA CLOTH & RAFFIA WEAVES. In the Congo and in other parts of Africa, raffia textiles were traditionally woven by women on a stationary vertical loom using fibers of the raffia-palm leaf. The weavings were in small pieces, then sewn together for bags, mats, and garments. Embroidery or appliqué was often added. Tapa — or beaten bark — cloth was and still is made in many parts of Africa and the Pacific regions by soaking and beating the bark of trees with paddles. Designs are applied by painting or stamping with pigments made of soot and red clay. Designs are also made by patchworking or embroidering with raffia.

LEFT. Raffia textiles woven in the Congo in the late 19th or early 20th Century. *Museum of Mankind — I–30.*

TOP. Tapa cloth with symbolic designs from New Guinea, 19–20th Century. *Museum of Mankind — XXV–5.*

BOTTOM. Tapa cloth from the Solomon Islands, 19–20th Century. *Museum of Mankind — XXV–2.*

RIGHT. Woven raffia pieces sewn together. The width is about 12 inches. *Museum of Mankind — I–1.*

TIE-DYE — IKAT — BATIK — 20TH CENTURY

LEFT. Silk tie-dyed cloth from India, probably early 20th Century. *V & A — FJ3275 (Circ 575–1965).*

RIGHT. Cotton tie-dyed cloth from Nigeria, early 20th Century. *Horniman Museum — 2300.*

TOP LEFT. Small detail of batik from Java, probably early 20th Century. *Museum of Mankind — 50011.*

TOP RIGHT. Detail of cotton double ikat from Bali, made about 1920. *V & A — FD2468 (IS13–1960).*

BOTTOM LEFT. Warp ikat from Borneo, probably early 20th Century. *Museum of Mankind — VIII–13.*

BOTTOM RIGHT. Tie-dye from the Ibo people, S. Nigeria, early 20th Century. *Museum of Mankind — LX–16.*

AFRICA — NARROW-STRIP WEAVING. The fabrics reproduced here illustrate three examples of African narrow-strip weaving. Similar cloths are woven in many parts of Africa by men on narrow horizontal looms which are portable. The men are professional weavers and carry their looms with them to execute commissions. This is in contrast to the wider women's looms, which are vertical, fixed, and used to make wider fabrics for family use. The narrow strips are joined together after weaving, and this type of construction has been in use on the Senegal coast since at least the mid-15th Century.

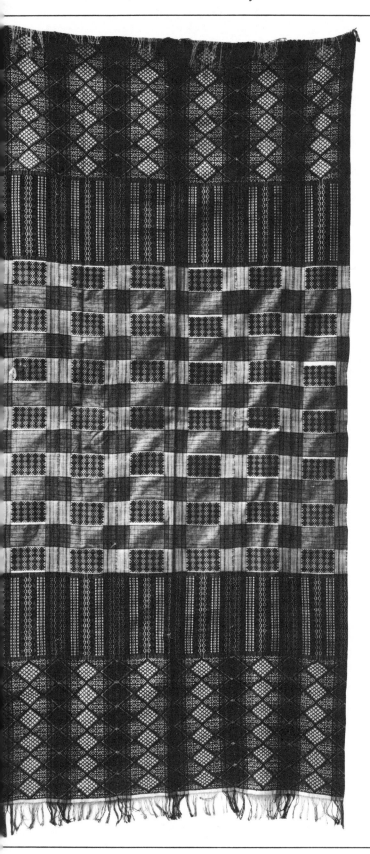

FAR LEFT. Narrow-strip men's weave in black and white from Upper Senegal, probably early 20th Century. To produce this cloth, six narrow strips were sewn together. *Museum of Mankind — 30274 (1934.3.7.197)*.

LEFT TOP & BOTTOM. Enlarged details of panel at left show the precision of this professional weaving.

RIGHT TOP. Another men's weave, this one made in Nigeria. *Museum of Mankind — XXXIII–19*.

RIGHT BOTTOM. A third men's weave from Upper Senegal. *Museum of Mankind — 30273 (1934.3.7.289)*.

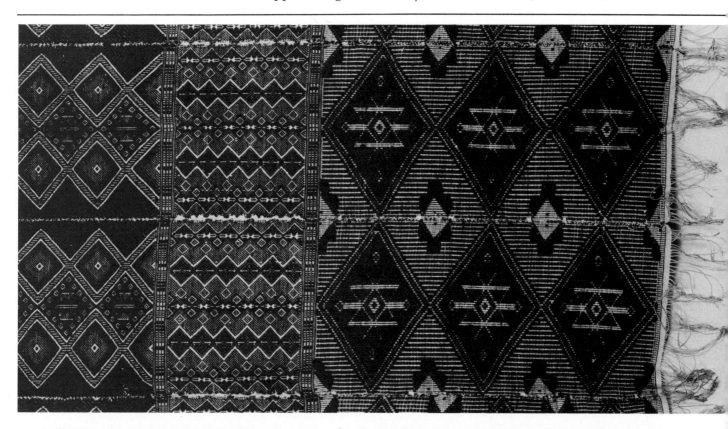

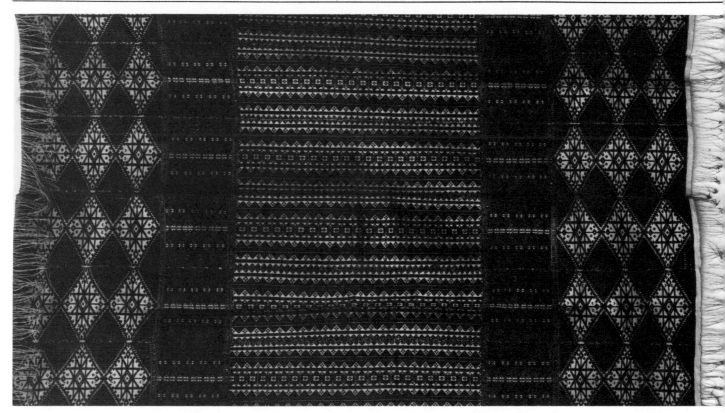

AFRICA — STAMP PRINTS & RESIST DYES. Two distinctive forms of applied decoration used in African textiles are the stamp print, called *adinkra*, and the cassava-paste resist dye, called *adire eleko*. Of the *adinkra* prints the best known are those of the Ashanti in Ghana (formerly the Gold Coast). Stamps are carved from calabash gourds, handles are attached, and the stamps are dipped in a bark dye and then pressed on the cloth. The designs are ideograms of folk sayings and concepts: for example, a ram's-horn symbol stands for strength. The *adire eleko* fabrics are made very much like batiks, using as resist a cassava paste with which the design is painted, often with a palm frond.

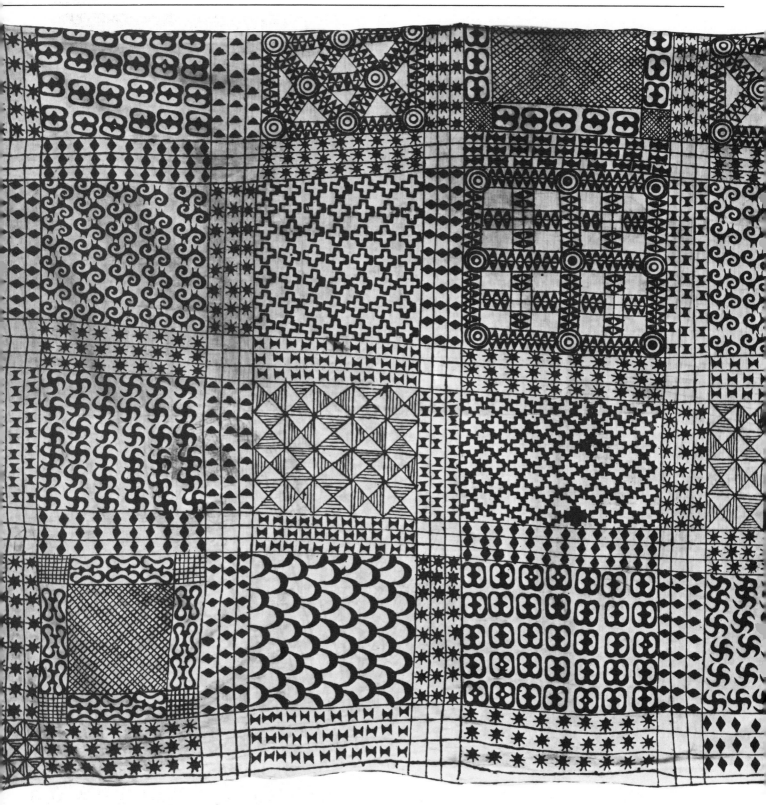

In recent times the designs have also been applied with stencils cut from zinc plates. A representative design is shown here.

LEFT. *Adinkra* cloth from the Gold Coast (now Ghana), early 20th Century. *Museum of Mankind — II–20.*

RIGHT. *Adire eleko*, a blue/white resist dye, Nigeria, early 20th Century. *Museum of Mankind — 10375.*

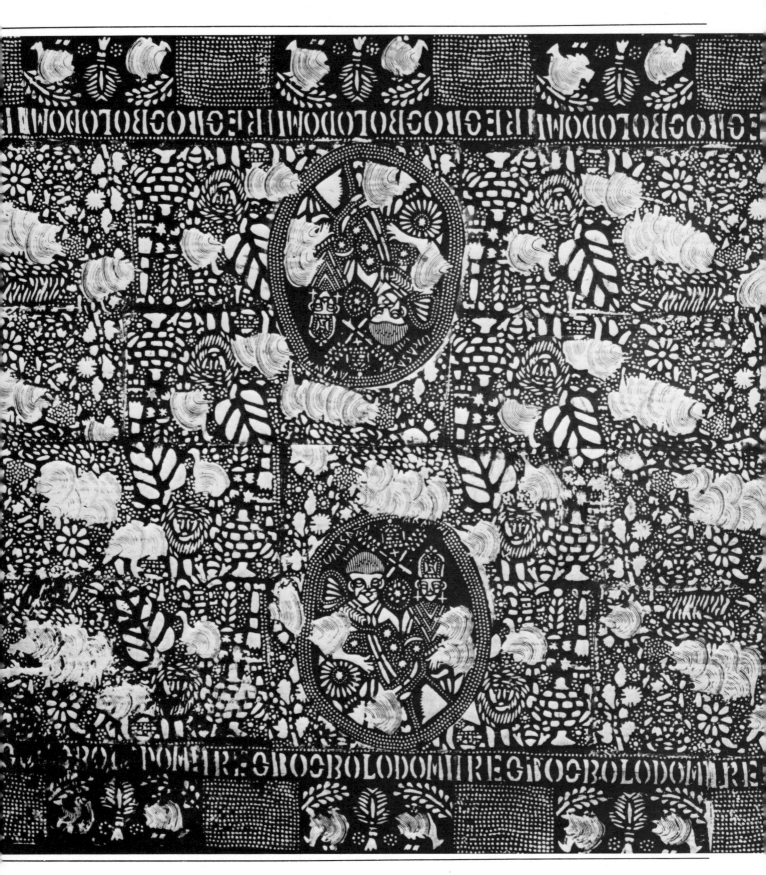

AFRICA — JUBILEE CLOTH. An intriguing example of the *adire eleko* resist-dye process is shown above. It is a commemorative "Jubilee" cloth made with a stencil but with the addition of other motifs applied with a comb dipped in dye. The figures within the circles are presumably those of the king and queen. The larger section of the design has evidently been made up with a single stencil, which has been reversed to give the fabric two directions. A detail from a different but similar "Jubilee" cloth is shown at the lower right on the facing page.

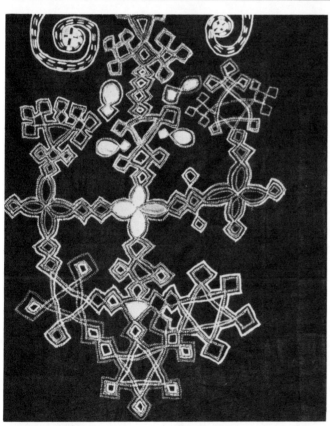

LEFT. *Adire eleko* ''Jubilee'' cloth from Nigeria, early 20th Century. *Museum of Mankind — 10395.*

TOP. Hand-painted, resist-dyed pattern from Nigeria, early 20th Century. *Museum of Mankind — LXXXIII–18.*

BOTTOM LEFT. Embroidered indigo shirt from Nigeria, early 20th Century. *Museum of Mankind — LXXX–16.*

BOTTOM RIGHT. Stenciled and combed design, Nigeria, 20th Century. *V & A — FJ3274 (Circ 756–1967).*

CONTEMPORARY TEXTILES — I. The commercial textiles of today play only a minor role in museum collections. That is understandable, though not excusable. Eligible contemporary fabrics are produced in such profusion today that they would quickly overtax the facilities of most museums. Moreover, little thought has been given to the method or the criteria to be used in selecting these fabrics, and no curator can be expected to know or evaluate all the fabrics produced in a fast-paced modern textile market. In spite of these obstacles, both the V & A and the Whitworth make an effort to keep a record of contemporary textile design.

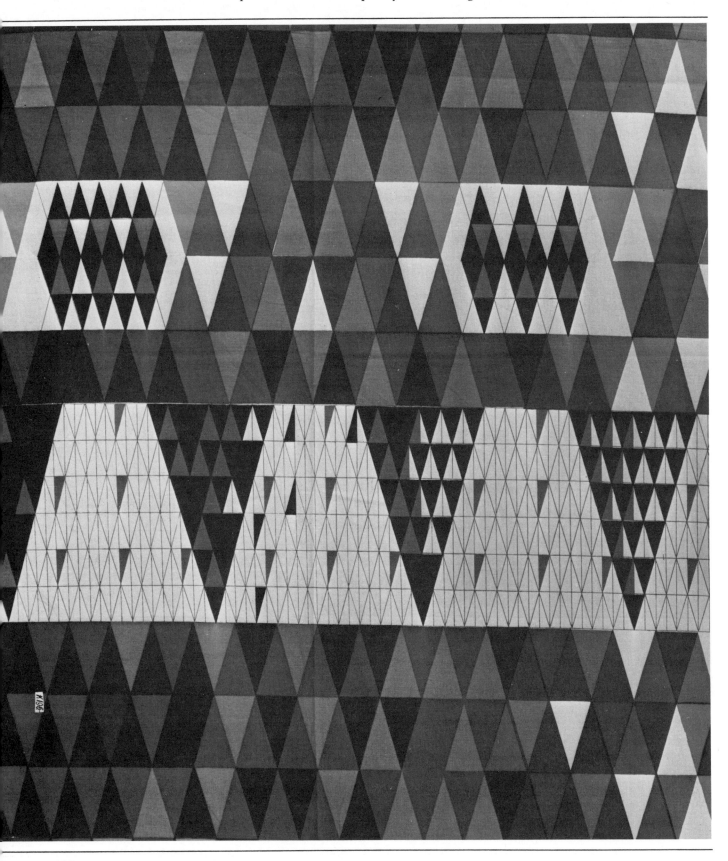

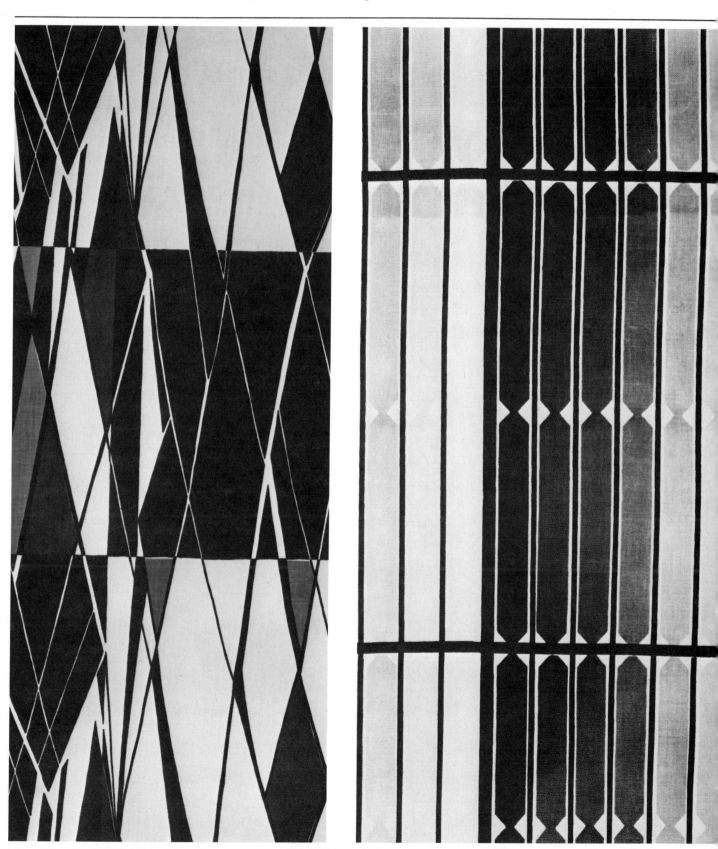

CONTEMPORARY TEXTILES — II

LEFT. French print by Raoul Dufy for Bianchini Ferrier, 1925. *V & A — GB3296 (Circ 113–1939).*

TOP. "Bartok," a Swedish screen-printed cotton by Hisse Stoog, 1956. *V & A — P319 (Circ 88–1956).*

BOTTOM. "May Time" (c. 1970), a printed furnishings fabric from *Kilkenny Design Workshops, Ireland.*

TOP. Finnish screen-printed cotton furnishing by Printex, 1956. *V & A — P325 (Circ 659–1956)*.

BOTTOM. Norwegian screen-printed rayon fabric by Hjura Veveri, 1956. *V & A — P324 (Circ 123–1956)*.

RIGHT. "Mona," a Swedish cotton screen print by K. Simmullar, 1956. *V & A — P320 (Circ 79–1956)*.

INDEX